ROBERT BURNS
The LASSIES

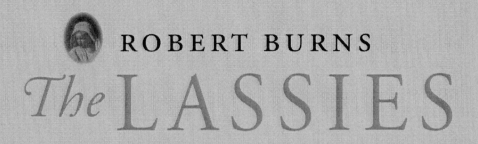

ROBERT BURNS
The LASSIES

GEORGE SCOTT WILKIE

NEIL WILSON PUBLISHING LIMITED · GLASGOW

Neil Wilson Publishing Ltd
303 The Pentagon Centre
36 Washington Street
GLASGOW
G3 8AZ

Tel: 0141-221-1117
Fax: 0141-221-5363
E-mail: info@nwp.co.uk
http://www.nwp.co.uk

First published February 2004
Reprinted April 2004, April 2005

A catalogue record for this book is available from the British Library.

ISBN 1-903238-65-X
Typeset in Adobe Jenson
Printed by Digisource

Contents

Introduction

I pray draw near and lend an ear,
And welcome in a Frater,
For I've lately been in quarantine,
A proven Fornicator.

Robert Burns wrote these words when his affair with Elizabeth Paton required him to answer to the Kirk Session and be punished. But were these the words of a true philanderer or simply the defiant response of an angry young man railing against an institution that he regarded as being totally out of touch with the real world? It is an undisputed fact that Robert Burns was fond of women. He loved to be in their company and his well-documented affairs have earned him a reputation as a rake and a womanizer.

Was this, however, a fair assessment of the man, or was it a reputation given by those puritanical people recognised by him so clearly in his poem, *Address to the Unco Guid*, and written to mock them? More recently, this reputation has been built upon by various writers, most of whom were born in the first half of the 20th century, probably the most sexually repressed period in the history of our nation. In the 1930s, Catherine Carswell, a very radical writer, produced a book in which she emphasised the sexual activities of Burns the man as opposed to Burns the writer. She was pilloried by the establishment of the time who tended to ignore that aspect of his life, believing that his words were of far more importance than his supposed sexual misdemeanours.

Nevertheless, this opened the floodgates for many writers who were keen to make their reputations by emphasising the negative side of his life and largely ignore his works. Sad to say, this aspect is still very much favoured by too many speakers at Burns Suppers, possibly because many of them are insufficiently familiar with his works to speak on them with any depth of knowledge. Quite frankly, young people today would wonder what on earth all the fuss was about.

The idea of Burns being a man without morals is highly arguable, as it is doubtful if his attitude towards sex was any different to most of his contemporaries. Robert Burns was a countryman and most of his liaisons were with like-minded country lassies who were only too familiar with the birds and the bees. In his *Sonnet Upon Sonnets*, he writes: 'Fourteen good years – a woman gives us life' not only indicating that childbirth was normal for young girls barely out of childhood themselves, but also giving us a clear picture that sex was part of life at an early age in the 18th century.

If one considers the level of immorality that was common throughout the British Isles at that time, perhaps Burns' behaviour was not quite so out of step with the rest of society as many choose to believe. London was then a cesspit of vice and drunkenness. Prostitution was one of the city's major industries and many of the fine old houses, particularly around the area of Covent Garden, were built upon the proceeds of a thriving vice trade. Gin was consumed like water and was known as 'Mother's ruin'. Illegitimate children were not uncommon, particularly among the poorer classes, and it was not unusual for the father of such a child to bring it home and raise it as a member of his family. This was probably a much cheaper option than making financial recompense to the child's mother.

So let us not judge Burns by the standards we might consider to be correct in today's society, but simply accept him for the beauty and genius of his words. His brother, Gilbert, stated later in life that Rab couldn't just admire a lass, he tended to fall head-over-heels in love with great ease and treated each of his young ladies as being the only love he ever knew. It is questionable if he approached a relationship with any cynical intent whatsoever. Attracted to women like a moth to a flame, he had an almost uncontrollable urge to love them and be loved by them.

As you read the poems and letters, you will realise that in Burns' eyes every woman he loved was a flawless beauty with an equally flawless character. For a man who had the most incredible ability to judge character, Burns wore rose-tinted spectacles where his women were concerned. His wife, Jean Armour, recognised her husband's failings and commented that 'Rab should hae twa wives'.

Burns may well have shared Jean's thoughts on that subject as he wrote later in life:

> That hackney'd judge of human life,
> The Preacher and the King,
> Observes; 'The man who gets a wife
> He gets a noble thing.'
>
> But how capricious are mankind,
> Now loathing, now desirous!
> We married men, how oft we find
> The best of things will tire us.

No, Robert Burns was no innocent, but he was one of the few men of his time who actually treated women as equals and did not regard them to be simply part of the household goods and chattels, as was too often the case at that time. His poem, *The Rights of Woman*, written well over a hundred years before women were eligible to vote in Great Britain, puts him among the champions of the feminist cause.

During his tragically short life Burns wrote many, many poems with a female as the focal point. Some are love poems or songs, obviously intended to sway the heart of whoever had caught his eye, while others are in honour of a more casual acquaintance whose beauty or talents had impressed him in some way or composed simply as a form of thank-you letter for gifts or hospitality that he may have received. In many, it is impossible to identify the subject, and one or two are verging on being unkind, even spiteful. *Robert Burns – The Lassies* has a common theme: that each poem or song is written to, or about, the women encountered by Robert Burns during his lifetime. Where possible, we find out a little of the background of these women who have been immortalised by their acquaintance with the Bard. I also include a few extracts from letters which have survived the years, written to or about some of the girls in his life. Not all of them are even real characters, simply names plucked at random for poetic purposes. However, let us not forget that there were other women in the life of Robert Burns who were not the subject of poems and songs. This book does not refer to them, only those mentioned in his songs and verses are included.

As well as being a poet, Robert Burns was a prolific writer of letters. Many of which were directed at young ladies who probably found other partners in life and to whom his letters may have been a source of embarrassment. Consequently, very few of them have survived throughout the ages, but those that have are wonderful to read and are written in a style far removed from his poetry. Composed in perfect English grammar, there is no trace of the auld Scots tongue so popular in his verses.

When you have read his poems, songs and letters, you may also come to believe that Robert Burns was no philanderer who preyed upon unsuspecting females, but that he was in fact a true romantic who could see little but beauty and charm in womanhood – a man who was so intense in his feelings that he truly believed himself to be in love with all of the women with whom he was associated. His ability to turn out passionate and flowery verse at the drop of a hat is incredible, particularly as each one is apparently written with the utmost sincerity.

But what of Burns the farmer, the scholar, the man of great compassion and devastating vitriol, the philosopher, the freedom fighter, the loving husband and doting father, the darling of the upper class and the champion of the working class, the writer of both romantic love songs and rude and bawdy songs, the lover of the beauty of nature and the hater of hunters, the scourge of hypocrisy, the man of deeply religious beliefs and the man who scorned the church and its preachers, the manic depressive and the arrogant, cocky fellow, the lover and seducer and the man who believed in equality for women, the man of sympathy and the man capable of terrible rudeness, the patriot whose greatest pride was in having been born a Scot, the internationally respected advocate for the freedom of all men? In the simplest of terms: Robert Burns, the genius. He was all of these, but here we have Burns, the admirer of women.

Contrary to popular belief, however, Burns' admiration for women was far from being swayed merely by a pretty face. He much preferred someone of intellect, for he was very aware that beauty is only skin-deep and short-lived.

> The charms o' the min' the langer they shine,
> The mair admiration they draw, man,
> While peaches and cherries, and roses and lilies,
> They fade and they wither awa' man.

This collection of poems and songs represents only a tiny fragment of Burns' body of work. Although we may find them of interest, he would have considered few of them to be of any great significance. However, several are of importance as they are written to, or about, young ladies who played a meaningful part in his life. Many of the others, although beautiful to read, would be dismissed by the Bard as mere trivia compared with his great masterpieces which have led to his immortal fame. Never let us forget that the driving force behind Burns was his constant battling for equality and freedom for all of mankind, irrespective of colour, race or creed.

Nelly Kilpatrick

We start with the very first poem written by young Rab at the tender age of 15. During harvest time it was normal practice for the field workers to be paired off. The strength of the male would be beneficial in gathering up the crops into stooks, while the nimble-fingered women would be more suitably employed in tying the stooks securely.

Young Rab's partner during this harvest was 14-year-old Nelly Kilpatrick, the daughter of a local farmer. Rab was smitten by Nell and in a letter written later in his life to Dr John Moore, he said:

This kind of life, the cheerless gloom of a hermit with the unceasing moil of a galley-slave, brought me to my sixteenth year, a little before which period I first committed the sin of RHYME. You know our country custom of coupling a man and a woman together as Partners in the labors of Harvest. In my fifteenth autumn, my partner was a bewitching creature who just counted an autumn less. My scarcity of English denies me the power of doing her justice in that language; but you know the Scotch idiom. She was a bonie, sweet, sonsie lass. In short, she altogether, unwittingly to herself, initiated me in a certain delicious Passion, which in spite of acid Disappointment, gin-horse Prudence and bookworm Philosophy, I hold to be the first of human joys, our dearest pleasure here below. How she caught the contagion I can't say; you medical people talk much of infection by breathing the same air, the touch &c, but I never expressly told her that I loved her. Indeed, I did not well know myself why I liked so much to loiter behind with her, when returning in the evening from our labours; why the tones of her voice made my heart-strings thrill like an Aeolian harp; and particularly why my pulse beat such a furious rantann, when I looked and fingered over her hand to pick out the nettle stings and thistles.

However, this admiration never progressed beyond the point of friendship and Nell had no further part in the life of the poet other than being the subject of what was to be his first recorded poem.

O, ONCE I LOV'D

O, once I lov'd a bonie lass,
An' aye I love her still,
An' whilst that virtue warms my breast
I'll love my handsome Nell.

As bonie lasses I hae seen,
And mony full as braw,
But for a modest gracefu' mien
The like I never saw.

A bonie lass I will confess,
Is pleasant to the e'e,
But without some better qualities
She's no a lass for me.

But Nelly's looks are blythe and sweet,
And what is best of a',
Her reputation is compleat,
And fair without a flaw.

She dresses ay sae clean and neat,
Both decent and genteel;
And then there's something in her gait
Gars ony dress look weel.

A gaudy dress and gentle air
May gently touch the heart,
But it's innocence and modesty
That polishes the dart.

'Tis this in Nelly pleases me,
'Tis this enchants my soul;
For absolutely in my breast
She reigns without controul.

braw = handsome; mien = demeanour; e'e = eye; gars = makes

Peggy Thomson

Burns, now 17, was spending a few weeks in summer studying at a school in Kirkoswald and was fixated by attractive young women. Again he wrote to his friend, Dr John Moore, stating:

> *A charming Filette who lived next door to the school overset my Trigonometry and set me off on a tangent from the sphere of my studies.*

The 'charming Filette' was Peggy Thomson, a young lady who eventually was to marry a friend of the Bard. Burns also uses this poem to voice his loathing of field sports.

SONG, COMPOSED IN AUGUST

Now wrestling winds, and slaught'ring guns
Bring Autumn's pleasant weather;
The moorcock springs on whirring wings,
Amang the blooming heather.
Now waving grain, wide o'er the plain,
Delights the weary Farmer;
The moon shines bright, as I rove at night,
To muse upon my Charmer.

The Pairtrick lo'es the fruitfu' fells;
The Plover lo'es the mountains;
The Woodcock haunts the lonely dells;
The soaring Hern the fountains
Thro' lofty groves the Cushat roves,
The path o' man to shun it;
The hazel bush o'erhangs the Thrush,
The spreading thorn the Linnet.

Thus ev'ry kind their pleasures find,
The savage and the tender;
Some social join, and leagues combine;
Some solitary wander:
Avaunt, away! the cruel sway,
Tyrannic man's dominion;
The Sportsman's joy, the murd'ring cry,
The flutt'ring, gory pinion!

But Peggy dear, the ev'ning's clear,
Thick flies the skimming Swallow;
The sky is blue, the fields in view,
All fading green and yellow:
Come let us stray our gladsome way,
And view the charms o' Nature;
The rustling corn, the fruited thorn,
And ilka happy creature.

We'll gently walk, and sweetly talk,
While the silent moon shines clearly;
I'll clasp thy waist and fondly prest,
Swear how I lo'e thee dearly;
Not vernal show'rs to budding flow'rs,
Not Autumn to the Farmer,
So dear can be, as thou to me,
My fair, my lovely Charmer!

wrestling = western; pairtrick = partridge; hern = heron; cushat = wood-pigeon; ilka = every

This is one of several farewells that Burns wrote prior to his proposed departure to the West Indies. The poem was directed to Peggy Thomson, his old sweetheart, who had since married a good friend of the Bard, but it is unclear to whom the letter was addressed.

'Twas the girl I mentioned in my letter to Dr Moore, where I speak of taking the sun's altitude – Poor Peggy! Her husband is my old acquaintance and a most worthy fellow. – When I was taking leave of my Carrick relations intending to go to the West Indies, when I took farewell of her, neither she nor I could speak a syllable. – Her husband escorted me three miles on my road, and we both parted with tears.

LINES WRITTEN TO AN OLD SWEETHEART

Once fondly lov'd, and still remembered dear,
Sweet early Object of my youthful vows,
Accept this mark of friendship, warm, sincere,
Friendship – 'tis all cold duty now allows.

And while you read the simple, artless rhymes,
One friendly sigh for him – he asks no more,
Who, distant, burns in flamin' torrid climes,
Or haply lies beneath th' Atlantic roar.

Agnes Fleming

These few verses are believed to have been written about Agnes Fleming, the daughter of a local farmer. Virtually nothing is known of any relationship that Burns may have had with this young lady, so perhaps she was simply someone upon whom the young poet was sharpening his rhyming skills.

MY NANIE, O.

Beyond yon hills where Lugar flows,
'Mang moors an' mosses many, O;
The wintry sun the day has clos'd,
And I'll awa to Nanie, O.

The wrestling wind blaws loud an' shrill;
The night's baith mirk and rainy, O;
But I'll get my plaid an' out I'll steal,
An' owre the hill to Nanie, O.

My Nanie's charming, sweet an' young;
Nae artfu' wiles to win ye, O;
May ill befa' the flattering tongue
That wad beguile my Nanie, O.

Her face is fair, her heart is true,
As spotless as she's bonie, O;
The op'ning gowan, wat wi' dew;
Nae purer is than Nanie, O.

A country lad is my degree,
An' few there are that ken me, O;
But what care I how few they be,
I'm welcome ay to Nanie, O.

My riches a's my penny-fee,
An' I maun guide it cannie, O;
But warl's gear ne'er troubles me,
My thoughts are a' my Nanie, O.

Our auld guidman delights to view
His sheep an' kye thrive bonie, O;
But I'm as blythe that hauds his pleugh,
An' hae nae care but Nanie, O.

Come weel come woe, I care na by,
I'll tak what Heav'n will sen' me, O;
Nae ither care in life have I,
But live, an' love my Nanie, O.

mosses = bogs; wrestling = western; baith = both; mirk = murky; gowan = daisy; wat = wet; ken = know; maun = must; cannie = careful; warl's gear = worldly goods; kye = cattle; hauds = holds; pleugh = plough; care na by = don't care

Isabella Steven

This poem is certainly directed at a young lady, but it is far from complimentary. Robert was by then learning that there was a gulf between the very rich and the very poor, and he did not like it one bit. This is the beginning of his railing against the inequality that such a gulf creates. Tibbie, or Isabella Steven, was the daughter of a rich, farming family and considered herself much too superior to associate with the poorly-clad Burns brothers.

The poet was 17 when he wrote these lines and you can feel the searing resentment pouring from his pen.

O TIBBIE, I HAE SEEN THE DAY

Chorus
O Tibbie, I hae seen the day,
Ye wadna be sae shy!
For laik o' gear ye lightly me,
But trowth I care na by!

Yestreen I met you on the Moor,
Ye spak' na but gaed by like stoor!
Ye geck at me because I'm poor –
But fient a hair care I!

When comin' home on Sunday last,
Upon the road as I cam' past,
Ye snufft an' gae your head a cast –
But trowth I care't na by!

I doubt na lass, but you may think
Because ye hae the name o' clink
That ye can please me at a wink
When e'er ye like to try:

But sorrow tak him that's sae mean,
Altho' his pouch o' coin were clean,
Wha follows ony saucy Quean
That looks sae proud and high!

Altho' a lad were e'er sae smart,
If that he want the yellow dirt,
Ye'll cast your head anither airt,
An answer him fu' dry.

But if he hae the name o' gear,
Ye'll fasten to him like a breer
Tho' hardly he for sense or lear;
    Be better than the kye.

But Tibbie, lass, tak' my advice
Your daddie's gear mak's you sae nice,
The Deil a ane wad spier your price,
    Were ye as poor as I.

There lives a lass beyond yon park,
I'd rather hae her in her sark,
Than you wi' a' your thousand mark,
    That gars ye look sae high.

wadna = would not; laik o' = lack of; gear = wealth; lightly = ignore; trowth = truth; gaed by = went by; stoor = dust; geck = scorn; clink = money; Quean = young girl; airt = direction; lear = learning; kye = cattle; spier = inquire; sark = shift; gars = makes

Annie

Burns either composed this song in 1782 or took an old ballad and rewrote it in his own style. We have no idea if the lass referred to in the song was real or fictional, but by this stage in his life the poet had moved away from shy modesty as being a necessity for any young lady to attract him. No matter, this song remains popular at any Burns gathering today.

THE RIGS O' BARLEY
CORN RIGS ARE BONIE

Chorus
Corn Rigs an' barley rigs,
An' corn rigs are bonie;
I'll ne'er forget that happy night
Amang the rigs wi' Annie.

It was upon a Lammas night,
When corn rigs are bonie,
Beneath the moon's unclouded light,
I held awa to Annie;
The time flew by, wi' tentless heed;
Till, 'tween the late and early,
Wi' sma' persuasion she agreed
To see me thro' the barley.

The sky was blue, the wind was still,
The moon was shining clearly;
I set her down, wi' right good will,
Amang the rigs o' barley;
I kent her heart was a' my ain;
I lov'd her most sincerely;
I kissed her owre and owre again,
Amang the rigs o' barley.

I lock'd her in my fond embrace;
Her heart was beating rarely:
My blessings on that happy place,
Amang the rigs o' barley!
But by the moon and stars so bright,
That shone that hour so clearly!
She ay shall bless that happy night
Amang the rigs o' barley.

I hae been blythe wi' comrades dear;
I hae been merry drinking;
I hae been joyfu' gath'ring gear,
I hae been happy thinking:
But a' the pleasures e'er I saw,
Tho' three times doubl'd fairly –
That happy night was worth them a',
Amang the rigs o' barley.

rigs = ridges; tentless = careless; kent = knew; owre = over; gath'ring gear = amassing wealth

Eliza

Burns historians are at odds with the identity of this young lady. One school of thought has her as Elizabeth Miller, one of the Mauchline Belles, while others point towards an Elizabeth Barbour.

However, there is a strong possibility that Eliza may well have been Elizabeth Paton, the serving girl who bore Burns' child, his 'Dear Bought Bess'.

This song gives an indication of the Bard's feeling that his future was not to be in his beloved Scotland, but in some far off place.

ELIZA

From thee, Eliza, I must go,
And from my native shore;
The cruel fates between us throw
A boundless ocean's roar;
But boundless oceans, roaring wide,
Between my Love and me,
They never, never can divide
My heart and soul from thee.

Farewell, farewell, Eliza dear;
The maid that I adore!
A boding voice is in mine ear,
We part to meet no more!
But the latest throb that leaves my heart,
While Death stands victor by,
That throb, Eliza, is thy part,
And thine that latest sigh!

Alison Begbie

The subject of this particular poem was Alison Begbie, also known as Elison, a servant girl from nearby Loudon. She so entranced the Bard that he made a formal proposal of marriage to her that she rejected. Possibly the reputation of the young poet was beginning to work against him, so he bombarded Alison with letters which appear to be an attempt to depict himself as a serious person, not the rake that he was considered to be.

This was in 1781, and it was 21-year-old Rab's first serious venture into a romance which he hoped would lead to marriage. But the letters he wrote to Alison were different to his poetry in that he almost appeared to be portraying himself as a very respectable, clean-living Christian. It almost seems as though he was using the letters as an exercise in writing, rather than epistles of true love and devotion.

The letters are too lengthy to include here, but one or two extracts show the amazing difference in Burns the poet and Burns the writer of letters.

He starts off in a very stilted manner apologizing for having taken the freedom to write in this manner, stressing to her that he is a stranger to the art of courtship.

I hope you will forgive me when I tell you that I most sincerely and affectionately love you. – I am a stranger in these matters Alison, and I assure you that you are the first woman to whom I ever made such a declaration, so I declare I am at a loss how to proceed.

He continues at a later date in a style which is far from romantic:

I verily believe, my dear E., that the pure genuine feelings of love, are as rare in the world as the pure genuine principles of virtue and piety.
This I hope will account for the uncommon style of all my letters to you. By uncommon, I mean that their being written in such a serious manner, which to tell you the truth, has made me often afraid lest you should take me for some zealous bigot, who conversed with his mistress as he would converse with his minister. I don't know how it is my dear; for though, except for your company, there is nothing on earth gives me so much pleasure as writing to you, yet it never gives me those giddy raptures so much talked of among lovers.

And carrying on in a similar vein:

E, you will do the justice to believe me, when I assure you, that the love I have for you is founded on the sacred principles of virtue and honour, and by consequences so long as you continue possessed of those amiable qualities which first inspired my passion for you, so long must I continue to love you. Believe me, my dear, it is love like this alone which can render the married state happy. People may talk of flame and raptures as long as they please; and a warm fancy, with a flow of youthful spirits, may make them feel something like what they describe; but sure I am, the nobler faculties of the mind with kindred feelings of the heart, can only be the foundation of friendship, and it has always been my opinion, that married life was only friendship in a more exalted degree.

No words of burning love for Alison, just an offer of friendship! Burns eventually wrote to Alison with a formal proposal of marriage:

There is one rule which I have hitherto practiced, and which I shall invariably keep with you, and that is, honestly to tell you the plain truth. There is something so mean and unmanly in the art of dissimulation and falsehood, that I am surprised they can be acted by anyone in so noble, so generous a passion as virtuous love. No, my dear E. I shall never endeavour to gain your favour by such detestable practices. If you will be so good and so generous as to admit me for your partner, your companion, your bosom friend through life; there is nothing on this side of eternity shall give me greater transport; but I shall never think of purchasing your hand by arts unworthy of a man, and I will add, of a Christian.

It seems that Alison did not relish the idea of being his bosom friend throughout her life for she rejected his offer of marriage. In a final letter, the spurned suitor wrote:

I ought in good manners to have acknowledged the receipt of your letter before this time, but my heart was so shocked with the contents of it, that I can scarcely yet collect my thoughts so as to write you on the subject.

He expressed the thought that he would never again meet anyone to whom he would be able to offer his love and affection again, and wrote the following poem, although it is unclear at what stage in the relationship the words were penned.

THE LASS O' CESSNOCK BANKS

On Cessnock banks a lassie dwells,
Could I describe her shape and mien!
Our lasses a' she far excels,
An' she has twa sparkling, rogueish een!

She's sweeter than the morning dawn
When rising Phoebus first is seen,
And dew-drops twinkle o'er the lawn;
An' she has twa sparkling, rogueish een!

She's stately, like yon youthful ash
That grows the cowslip braes between,
And drinks the stream with vigour fresh;
An' she has twa sparkling, rogueish een!

She's spotless, like the flow'ring thorn,
With flow'rs so white and leaves so green,
When purest in the dewy morn;
An' she has twa sparkling, rogueish een!

Her looks are like the vernal May,
When ev'ning Phoebus shines serene,
Where birds rejoice on every spray,
An' she has twa sparkling, rogueish een!

Her hair is like the curling mist
That climbs the mountain-sides at e'en,
When flow'r-reviving rains are past,
An' she has twa sparkling, rogueish een!

Her forehead's like the show'ry bow
When gleaming sunbeams intervene,
And gild the distant mountain's brow,
An' she has twa sparkling, rogueish een!

Her cheeks are like yon crimson gem,
The pride of all the flowery scene,
Just opening on its thorny stem;
An' she has twa sparkling, rogueish een!

Her teeth are like the nightly snow
When pale the morning rises keen,
While hid the murm'ring streamlets flow,
An' she has twa sparkling, rogueish een!

Her lips are like yon cherries ripe
Which sunny walls from Boreas screen;
They tempt the taste and charm the sight;
An' she has twa sparkling, rogueish een!

Her breath is like the fragrant breeze
That gently stirs the blossom'd bean,
When Phoebus sinks below the seas;
An' she has twa sparkling, rogueish een!

But it's not her air, her form, her face,
Tho' matching Beauty's fabled Queen;
'Tis the mind that shines in ev'ry grace –
An' chiefly in her rogueish een!

een = eyes; braes = hills

Montgomerie's Peggy

Following his rejection by Alison Begbie, Burns had gone to the town of Irvine to attempt to learn the trade of flax-dressing. Strange tales emanate from this period in his life. An association with a woman who belonged to a sect that believed in the practice of free love is mentioned by some historians.

Irvine was a disaster in the life of the Bard. The result of his venture into the flax-dressing business was financial ruin and ill-health. His business partner was dishonest and to cap his problems, their premises burnt to the ground while celebrating the New Year.

At 23 years old, Burns returned to the life of a farmer and apparently began to actively seek a wife.

Young Rab soon attempted courtship with the housekeeper of a local family, the Montgomeries, but she was already engaged and the romance was a very one-sided affair, so he was left alone once again.

He wrote:

My Montgomerie's Peggy was my Deity for six or eight months. She has been bred ... In a style of life rather elegant ... A vanity of showing my parts in Courtship ... made me lay siege to her; and when, as I always do in my foolish gallantries, I had battered myself into a warm affection for her, she told me ... that her fortress had been for some time the rightful property of another.

Altho' my bed were in yon muir,
Amang the heather, in my plaidie,
Yet happy, happy would I be
Had I my dear Montgomerie's Peggy.

When o'er the hills beat surly storms,
And winter nights were dark and rainy;
I'd seek some dell, and in my arms
I'd shelter dear Montgomerie's Peggy.

Were I a Baron proud and high,
And horse and servants waiting ready,
Then a' 'twad gi'e o' joy to me,
The sharin't with Montgomerie's Peggy.

muir = moor; 'twad gi'e = would give

Mary Morison

The historians are again at odds over the identity of this young lady. Some believe the song to have been dedicated to a 14-year-old girl living in Mauchline who died of consumption at the age of 20 and whose tombstone remains today in the Mauchline churchyard. Others doubt that the poet would have been seriously interested in one so young, pointing out that this was not an uncommon name and could have been someone unknown to us.

Yet another school of thought believes the song to have really been about Alison Begbie, simply given another name to disguise the Bard's feelings. At any rate, it is a lovely song describing the feelings of the lovesick swain who only has eyes for his true love. It has survived the passage of time and remains a favourite at any gathering where the poems and songs of Robert Burns are aired.

O Mary at thy window be,
It is the wish'd, the tryst'd hour,
Those smiles and glances let me see,
That makes the miser's treasure poor.
How blithely wad I bide the stoure,
A weary slave frae sun to sun,
Could I the rich reward secure –
The lovely Mary Morison!

Yestreen, when to the trembling string
The dance gaed thro' the lighted ha',
To thee my fancy took its wing,
I sat, but neither heard, nor saw;
Tho' this was fair, and that was braw,
And yon the toast of a' the town,
I sigh'd, and said amang them a',
'Ye are na Mary Morison!'

O, Mary, canst thou wreck his peace
Wha for your sake wad gladly die?
Or canst thou break that heart of his
Whase only faute is loving thee?
If love for love thou wilt na gi'e,
At least be pity to me shown;
A thought ungentle canna be
The thought o' Mary Morison.

bide the stoure = bear the struggle; yestreen = last evening; gaed = went; faute = fault; gi'e = give

Jean and Anna Ronald

William Ronald, his wife and two daughters, Jean and Anna, lived on a 200-acre farm near Tarbolton. Robert and his brother Gilbert appear to have been on good terms with the girls, but not good enough to be considered as suitors. In fact Gilbert courted the elder of the two, Jean, but to no avail. Robert's poem shows quite a strong feeling of resentment, as the brothers were considered too poor to be of interest to the Ronalds. Young ladies of both wealth and beauty were obviously a great attraction to many of the local bachelors, and in one letter Burns was rather cynical when he wrote to his friend, John Tennant, in September 1784:

> We talk of air & manner, of beauty & wit, and lord knows what unmeaning nonsense; but – there – is solid charms for you – Who would not be in raptures with a woman that will make him 300 pounds richer? And then to have a woman to lye with him when one pleases without running any risk of the cursed experience of bastards and all the other concomitants of that species of Smuggling – These are solid views of matrimony.

Nevertheless, this poem emphasises how Burns considered beauty to be merely skin deep, and how he would prefer to spend time with a woman of intelligence rather than of simple beauty.

THE RONALDS O' THE BENNALS

In Tarbolton, ye ken, there are proper young men,
And proper young lassies and a', man;
But ken ye the Ronalds that live in the Bennals?
They carry the gree for them a', man.

Their father's a laird, and weel he can spar't,
Braid money to tocher them a', man
To proper young men, he'll clink in the hand
Gowd guineas a hundred or twa, man.

There's ane they ca' Jean, I'll warrant ye've seen
As bonie a lass or as braw, man;
But for sense and guid taste, she'll vie wi' the best,
And a conduct that beautifies a', man

The charms o' the min', the langer they shine
The mair admiration they draw, man;
While peaches and cherries, and roses and lilies,
They fade and they wither awa', man.

If ye be for Miss Jean, tak this frae a frien',
   A hint o' a rival or twa, man,
The Laird o' Blackbyre wad gang through the fire,
   If that wad entice her awa, man.

The Laird o' Braehead has been on his speed,
   For mair than a towmond or twa, man;
The Laird o' the Ford will straught on a board,
   If he canna get her at a', man.

Then Anna comes in, the pride o' her kin,
   The boast of our bachelors a', man;
Sae sonsy and sweet, sae fully complete,
   She steals our affections awa', man.

If I should detail the pick and the wale
   O' lasses that live here awa', man;
The faut wad be mine, if she didna shine
   The sweetest and best o' them a', man.

I lo'e her mysel', but darena weel tell,
   My poverty keeps me in awe, man;
For making o' rhymes, and working at times,
   Does little or naething at a', man.

Yet I wadna choose to let her refuse
   Nor hae't in her power to say na, man;
For though I be poor, unnotic'd, obscure,
   My stomach's as proud as them a', man.

Though I canna ride in weel-booted pride,
   And flee o'er the hills like a craw, man,
I can haud up my head wi' the best o' the breed,
   Though fluttering ever so braw, man.

My coat and my vest, they are Scotch o' the best;
   O' pairs o' guid breeks I hae twa, man,
And stockings and pumps to put on my stumps,
   And ne'er a wrang steek in them a' man.

My sarks they are few, but five o' them new,
Twal'-hundred, as white as the snaw, man!
A ten-shillings hat, a Holland cravat –
There are no monie poets sae braw, man!

I never had freen's weel stockit in means,
To leave me a hundred or twa, man;
Nae weel-tochered aunts, to wait on their drants,
And wish them in hell for it a', man.

I never was cannie for hoardin' o' money,
Or claughtin 't together at a', man;
I've little to spend and naething to lend,
But devil a shilling I awe, man.

ken = know; carry the gree = bear the bell; braid = broad; tocher = dowry; gowd = gold; wad gang = would go; towmond = 12 months; straught = stretch; sonsy = pleasant; wale = choice; here awa' = around here; faut = fault; wadna = would not; hae't = have it; breeks = breeches; steek = stitch; sarks = shirts; weel stockit in means = wealthy; weel-tochered = well-endowed; cannie = careful; claughtin = clutching; awe = owe

However, things did not continue to go well for the wealthy Ronalds. William Ronald was to be declared bankrupt in 1789, and Burns wrote to his brother Gilbert:

Mr William Ronald is bankrupt. You will easily guess, that from his insolent vanity in his sunshine of life, he will feel a little retaliation from those who thought themselves eclipsed by him, for, poor fellow, I do not think he ever intentionally injured anyone. I might indeed perhaps except his wife, whom he has certainly used very ill ...

The Belles o' Mauchline

This is the first mention in verse of Jean Armour, who was eventually to become Burns' wife and who was to be featured so largely in his life.

Burns was impressed by the local young ladies, but one must wonder if there might be a hint of exaggeration in his description of these girls. But there again, beauty is in the eye of the beholder.

> In Mauchline there dwells six proper young Belles,
> The pride o' the place and its neighbourhood a',
> Their carriage and dress a stranger would guess,
> In Lon'on or Paris they'd gotten it a':
>
> Miss Miller is fine, Miss Murkland's divine,
> Miss Smith she has wit and Miss Betty is braw;
> There's beauty and fortune to get wi' Miss Morton,
> But Armour's the jewel for me o' them a'.

All Girls

A little bit of advice from Burns to the girls: be careful about reading novels for they may fire up your blood and imagination to a level where you will be easy prey for a rake such as he.

O LEAVE NOVELS

O leave novels, ye Mauchline belles,
Ye're safer at your spinning wheel;
Such witching books are baited hooks
For rakish rooks like Rob Mossgiel.

Your fine Tom Jones and Grandisons
They make your youthful fancies reel;
They heat your brains, and fire your veins,
And then you're prey for Rob Mossgiel.

Beware a tongue that's smoothly hung;
A heart that warmly seems to feel;
That feelin' heart but acks a part,
'Tis rakish art in Rob Mossgiel.

The frank address, the soft caress,
Are worse than poisoned darts of steel.
The frank address, and politesse,
Are all finesse in Rob Mossgiel.

All Women

This delightful old song is not in praise of any particular lass, but of womanhood in general. The last verse describes just how Robert Burns perceived women as being the darlings of Nature.

GREEN GROW THE RASHES

Chorus
Green grow the rashes, O;
Green grow the rashes, O;
The sweetest hours that e'er I spend,
Are spent among the lasses, O.

There's nought but care on ev'ry han',
In ev'ry hour that passes, O;
What signifies the life o' man,
An' 'twere na for the lasses, O?

The warl'ly race may riches chase,
An' riches still may fly them, O;
An' tho' at last they catch them fast,
Their hearts can ne'er enjoy them, O.

But gi'e me a canny hour at e'en,
My arms about my Dearie, O;
An' warl'ly cares, an' warl'ly men,
May a' gae tapsalteerie, O.

For you sae douce, ye sneer at this,
Ye're nought but senseless asses, O;
The wisest Man the warl' e'er saw,
He dearly lov'd the lasses, O.

Auld Nature swears the lovely Dears
Her noblest work she classes, O;
Her prentice han' she tried on man,
An' then she made the lasses, O.

warl'ly = worldly; gi'e = give; tapsalteerie = topsy-turvy; douce = sober

When he had completed this song, Burns wrote:

*I do not see that the turn of mind, and pursuits of such a one as the above verses describe –
One who spends the hours and thoughts which the vocations of the day can spare with
Ossian, Shakespeare, Sterne &c, or as the maggot takes him, a gun, a fiddle, or a Song to
make, or mend; and at all times some hearts-dear lass in view – are in the least more
inimical to the sacred interests of Piety and Virtue, than the, even lawful, bustling, and straining
after the worlds riches and honors: and I do not see but he may gain Heaven as well.*

He couldn't see why any scholar should deprive himself of the fun to be found with
the girls.

Elizabeth Paton

In my introduction I claimed that Robert Burns was a true romantic as opposed to a cynical user of women, although it would seem that his affair with Elizabeth Paton was the exception to the rule. She was a servant girl employed in the Burns' household and became pregnant by the Bard. His mother was of the opinion that Robert should marry Elizabeth, also more commonly known as Bess, but the rest of the family fought against this as they considered Bess to be too vulgar and unsophisticated for Robert.

This poem could hardly be described as a loving ditty, but as I am committed to extracting all his poems and songs with a female as the central character, this must be included.

MY GIRL SHE'S AIRY

My girl she's airy, she's buxom and gay,
Her breath is as sweet as the blossoms in May;
A touch of her lips it ravishes quite,
She's always good natur'd, good humor'd and free;
She dances, she glances, she smiles with a glee;
Her eyes are the lightenings of joy and delight;
Her slender neck, her handsome waist,
Her hair well buckl'd, her stays well lac'd,
Her taper white leg with an et, and a, c,
For her a, b, e, d, and her c, u, n, t,
And Oh, for the joys of a long winter night!!!

Rab and Elizabeth Paton were summoned to appear before the congregation to be publicly chastised for their sins, but, as the following poem demonstrates so clearly, Rab took his punishment with a very large pinch of salt and the pair continued with their affair on the way home from their supposed punishment.

He was proud to stand by his partner when she became pregnant, and used these verses to pour scorn upon any male who used the services of a prostitute, warning them of the dangers of contracting disease from such girls. But he also looks back in history at the many famous people who enjoyed the company of women and decides that they are really no different to himself.

Although Elizabeth Paton gave birth to a daughter, Burns chooses to describe a son in the poem, possibly for ease of rhyming.

THE FORNICATOR

Ye jovial boys who love the joys,
The blissful joys of Lovers;
Yet dare avow with dauntless brow,
When the bonie lass discovers;
I pray draw near and lend an ear,
And welcome in a Frater,
For I've lately been on quarantine,
A proven Fornicator.

Before the Congregation wide
I pass'd the muster fairly,
My handsome Betsey by my side,
We gat our ditty rarely;
But my downcast eye by chance did spy
What made my lips to water,
Those limbs so clean, where I, between,
Commenc'd a Fornicator.

With rueful face and signs of grace
I pay'd the buttock-hire,
The night was dark and thro' the park
I could not but convoy her;
A parting kiss, what could I less,
My vows began to scatter,
My Betsey fell – lal de lal lal,
I am a Fornicator.

But for her sake this vow I make,
And solemnly I swear it,
That while I own a single crown,
She's welcome for to share it;
And my roguish boy his Mother's joy,
And the darling of his Pater,
For him I boast my pains and cost,
Although a Fornicator.

Ye wenching blades whose hireling jades
Have tipt you off blue-boram,
I tell ye plain, I do disdain
To rank you in the Quorum;

But a bonie lass upon the grass
To teach her esse Mater,
And no reward but for regard,
O that's a Fornicator.

Your warlike Kings and Heroes bold,
Great Captains and Commanders;
Your mighty Caesars fam'd of old,
And Conquering Alexanders;
In fields they fought and laurels bought
And bulwarks strong did batter,
But still they grac'd our our noble list
And ranked Fornicators!!!

the bonie lass discovers = finds herself pregnant; Frater = brother; ditty = sermon; buttock-hire = a fine imposed by the kirk upon fornicators; convoy = accompany; hireling jades = prostitutes; tipt you off blue-boram = passed on venereal disease; esse Mater = be a mother

In his *Epistle to John Rankine*, Burns adopts an almost boastful attitude about this episode, comparing Elizabeth to a partridge he had shot down. He tells Rankine just how he intends to get his money's worth out of Elizabeth even if it means him having to flee the country and become a drover in America.

'Twas ae night lately, in my fun,
I gaed a rovin' wi' the gun,
An' brought a pairtrick to the grun' –
A bonie hen;
And, as the twilight was begun,
Thought nane wad ken.

The poor wee thing was little hurt;
I straikit it a wee for sport,
Ne'er thinkin' they wad fash me for't;
But Deil-ma-care!
Somebody tells the Poacher-Court
The hale affair.

Some auld, us'd hands hae ta'en a note,
That sic a hen had got a shot;
I was suspected for the plot;
I scorn'd to lie;
So gat the whissle o' my groat,
An' pay't the fee.

But by my gun, o' guns the wale,
An' by my pouther an' my hail,
An' by my hen an' by her tail.
I vow an' swear!
The game shall pay, owre moor an' dale,
For this niest year!

As soon's the clockin-time is by,
An' the wee powts begun to cry,
Lord, I'se hae sportin' by an' by
For my gowd guinea;
Tho' I should herd the buckskin kye
For't in Virginia.

pairtrick = partridge; grun = ground; straikit it a wee = stroked it a little; fash = worry; Poacher-Court = Kirk Session; gat the whissle o' my groat = lost my money; wale = pick; pouther an' my hail = powder and shot; niest = next; clockin-time = incubation period; powts = chicks; gowd = gold; buckskin kye = longhorn cattle

His Daughter Bess

Elizabeth Paton had become pregnant by Robert Burns and baby Elizabeth was the issue of this relationship. When the child was born, the Bard's mother took her into the household and raised her as a member of the family. This was common practice in those days when a young man found himself the father of an illegitimate child. The other option was financial recompense, but few working-class families could afford it, so the child was much more likely to become a family member. Robert Burns adored his daughter Bess, and promised her that she would never suffer from the stigma of being the product of unmarried parents.

This poem brings out the true compassion that was to make Burns such a revered figure throughout the world.

WELCOME TO A BASTART WEAN
A POET'S WELCOME TO HIS LOVE-BEGOTTEN DAUGHTER

Thou's welcome wean! mischanter fa' me,
If thoughts o' thee, or yet thy mammie,
Shall ever daunton me or awe me,
My bonie lady,
Or if I blush when thou shal't ca' me
Tyta, or daddie!

Tho' now they ca' me fornicator,
An' tease my name in kintra clatter,
The mair they talk, I'm kend the better,
E'en let them clash!
An auld wife's tongue's a feckless matter
To gi'e ane fash.

Welcome! My bonie, sweet, wee dochter!
Tho' ye came here a wee unsought for;
And thro' your coming I hae fought for
Baith kirk and queir;
Yet by my faith, ye're no unwrought for –
That I shall swear!

Sweet fruit o' monie a merry dint,
My funny toil is no' a' tint,
Tho' thou cam to the warl' asklent,
Which fools may scoff at
In my last plack thy part's be in it
The better half o't.

28

Tho' I should be the waur bestead,
Thou's be as braw and bienly clad,
And thy young years as nicely bred,
Wi' education,
As onie brat o' wedlock's bed,
In a' thy station.

Wee image o' my bonie Betty;
As fatherly I kiss and daut thee,
As dear an' near my heart I set thee
Wi' as guid will,
As a' the priests had seen me get thee
That's out o' Hell.

Gude grant that thou may ay inherit
Thy mither's looks an' gracefu' merit
An' thy poor, worthless daddie's spirit,
Without his failin's!
'Twill please me mair to see thee heir it,
Than stockit mailins.

And if thou be what I wad hae thee
And tak the counsel I shall gi'e thee,
I'll never rue my troubles wi' thee –
The cost nor shame o't,
But be a loving father to thee,
And brag the name o't.

wean = child; mischanter = misfortune; daunton = subdue; awe = awe; Tyta = father; kintra clatter = country gossip; mair = more; kend = known; clash = idle talk; auld wife = old woman; feckless = powerless; gi'e ane fash = give one trouble; dochter = daughter; kirk and queir = church and court; unwrought = unwanted; monie = many; dint = liaison; a' tint = all lost; warl' = world; asklent = obliquely; plack = small coin; waur = worse; bestead = position; braw = beautiful; bienly = comfortably; onie brat o' wedlock's bed = legitimate child; daut = dote; Gude = God; stockit mailin = well-stocked farm

Coila

This is not strictly a poem about one of his lady loves, but a wonderful example of just how Burns considered the good things in life to be female. *The Vision* is a lengthy poem in which Burns extols the beauty of the Scottish countryside and gives praise to her many great heroes and scholars. He does this through the medium of his Muse, who he describes as a beautiful young maiden. I have extracted those verses in which he describes her and it starts when he is sitting contemplating just what life has in store for him.

THE VISION

When click! the string the snick did draw;
And jee! the door gaed to the wa';
And by my ingle-lowe I saw,
Now bleezin bright,
A tight, outlandish hizzie, braw,
Come full in sight.

Ye need na doubt, I held my whisht;
The infant aith, half-form'd, was crush't;
I glowr'd as eerie's I'd been dusht,
In some wild glen;
When sweet, like some modest Worth, she blush't,
And stepped ben.

Green, slender, leaf-clad holly-boughs
Were twisted, gracefu', round her brows,
I took her for some Scottish Muse,
By that same token;
And come to stop those reckless vows,
Would soon been broken.

A 'hare-brain'd, sentimental trace'
Was strongly marked in her face;
A wildly-witty, rustic grace
Shone full upon her;
Her eye, ev'n turn'd on empty space,
Beam'd keen with honor.

Down flow'd her robe, a tartan sheen,
Till half a leg was scrimply seen,
And such a leg! my bonie Jean
Could only peer it;
Sae straught, sae taper, tight and clean,
Nane else came near it.

snick = door-latch; ingle-lowe = flame from the fire; bleezin = blazing; hizzie = young woman; held my whisht = kept quiet; glowr'd = stared; dusht = touched; ben = through; scrimply = barely; peer = equal

Margaret Kennedy

Young Peggy, as Margaret Kennedy was known, met Robert Burns at the home of Gavin Hamilton, Burns' good friend. There is no suggestion of any romantic link between Peggy and Burns, but Burns was pleased to send her this poem in tribute. Unfortunately, the good fortune that Burns wished the girl in the poem was not to be.

Peggy was seduced by an army captain and bore him a daughter. The captain refused to acknowledge the child and the affair was taken to court where it was decreed that the child was indeed the product of a legal marriage. Peggy was awarded a substantial sum of money from the court for the upbringing of the child, but sadly died at the age of 29 while the court action was being fought. The Bard's good wishes for her happy life were unfulfilled.

YOUNG PEGGY

Young Peggy blooms our boniest lass,
    Her blush is like the morning,
The rosy dawn, the springing grass,
    With early gems adorning.
Her eyes outshine the radiant beams
    That gild the passing shower,
And glitter o'er the crystal streams,
    And cheer each fresh'ning flower.

Her lips, more than the cherries bright,
    A richer dye has graced them;
They charm th' admiring gazer's sight,
    And sweetly tempt to taste them.
Her smile is as the ev'ning mild,
    When feather'd pairs are courting,
And little lambkins wanton wild,
    In playful bands disporting.

Were Fortune lovely Peggy's foe,
    Such sweetness would relent her,
As blooming Spring unbends the brow,
    Of surly, savage Winter.
Detraction's eye no aim can gain
    Her winning powers to lessen,
And fretful Envy grins in vain,
    The poison'd tooth to fasten.

Ye Pow'rs of Honour, Love, and Truth,
From ev'ry ill defend her!
Inspire the highly favour'd youth
The destinies intend her!
Still fan the sweet connubial flame
Responsive in each bosom;
And bless the dear parental name
With many a filial blossom.

Jenny

This is an extract from one of the most beautiful poems written by Robert Burns. It is the story of a working family who join together on a Saturday evening when their work is finished for the week. A very small part of this world-famous poem is included in this book as it demonstrates the amazing perception that Burns had of life.

These few verses describe the emotions running through young Jenny as her suitor is brought in to meet her family for the first time.

Once again we have a situation that is as pertinent today as when it was written all these years ago.

THE COTTER'S SATURDAY NIGHT

But hark! a rap comes gently to the door;
Jenny, wha kens the meaning o' the same.
Tells how a neebor lad came o'er the muir,
To do some errands, and convoy her hame.
The wily mother sees the conscious flame
Sparkle in Jenny's e'e, and flush her cheek,
With heart-struck, anxious care enquires his name,
While Jenny hafflins is afraid to speak;
Weel-pleas'd the Mother hears it's nae wild, worthless rake.

With kindly welcome, Jenny brings him ben;
A strappin youth, he takes the Mother's eye;
Blythe Jenny sees the visit's no ill ta'en;
The Father cracks of horses, pleughs and kye.
The youngster's artless heart o'erflows wi' joy,
But blate and laithfu', scarce can weel behave;
The Mother, wi' a woman's wiles, can spy
What makes the youth sae bashfu' and sae grave;
Weel-pleas'd to think her bairn's respected like the lave.

O happy love! where love like this is found;
O heart-felt raptures! bliss beyond compare!
I've paced much this weary, mortal round,
And sage experience bids me this declare –
'If Heaven a draught of heavenly pleasure spare,
One cordial in this melancholy vale,
'Tis when a youthful, loving, modest pair
In other's arms breathe out the tender tale,
Beneath the milk-white thorn that scents the ev'ning gale.'

Is there, in human form, that bears a heart –
A wretch! a villain! lost to love and truth!
That can, wi' studied, sly, ensnaring art,
Betray sweet Jenny's unsuspecting youth?
Curse on his perjur'd arts! dissembling, smooth!
Are honour, virtue, conscience, all exil'd?
Is there no pity, no relenting ruth,
Points to the parent fondling o'er their child?
Then paints the ruin'd maid, and their distraction wild?

wha kens = who knows; cam o'er = came over; hafflins = half; rake = waster; ben = through; no ill ta'en = not ill-taken; cracks = talks; kye = cattle; blate and laithfu' = sheepish and bashful; the lave = the others; perjur'd arts = lies; dissembling = masking;   ruth = remorse

Wilhelmina Alexander

This particular 'Bonie Lass' was Wilhelmina Alexander, born in 1756, and daughter of a local laird. Burns happened upon her one evening when walking and was so infatuated by her beauty that he wrote her a letter and sent it along with a song composed in her honour. The song is one of many that are still sung today, so many years after it was written. And let's not forget that Burns had not even spoken to Wilhelmina. None of his many beautiful songs and poems depict the Bard as a hopeless romantic more so than this futile pursuit of a woman he did not know, but fell in love with at a single glance.

Miss Alexander chose to ignore the poet's advances but nevertheless kept the poem and letter in her possession until her death in 1843.

He wrote:

Mossgiel, 18th November, 1786

Madam,

Poets are such outré Beings, so much the children of wayward Fancy and capricious Whim, that I believe the world generally allows them a larger latitude in the rules of Propriety, than the sober sons of Judgement and Prudence. – I mention this as an apology all at once for the liberties which a nameless Stranger has taken with you in the inclosed; and which he begs leave to present you with.

Whether it has poetical merit in any way worthy of the THEME, I am not the proper judge, but it is the best my abilities can produce; and what to a good heart will always be a superiour grace, it is equally sincere. –

The scenery was nearly taken from real life; though I dare say, Madam, you don't recollect it: for I believe you scarcely noticed the poetic Reveur, as he wandered by you. – I had roved out as Chance directed on the favourite haunts of my Muse, the banks of Ayr; to view Nature in all the gayety of the vernal year. –

The sun was flaming o'er the distant, western hills; not a breath stirred the crimson opening blossom, or the verdant spreading leaf.

'Twas a golden moment for a poetic heart. – I listened the feathered Warblers, pouring their harmony on every hand, with a congenial, kindred regard; and frequently turned out of my path lest I should disturb their little songs, or frighten them to another station. –

'Surely,' said I to myself, 'he must be a wretch indeed, who, regardless of your harmonious endeavours to please him, can eye your elusive flights, to discover your secret recesses, and rob you of all the property Nature gives you; your dearest comforts, your helpless, little Nestlings.' Even the hoary Hawthorn twig that shot across the way, what heart, at such a time, but must have been interested in its welfare, and wished it to be preserved from the rudely browsing Cattle, or the withering eastern Blast?

Such was the scene, and such the hour, when in a corner of my prospect I spyed one of the finest pieces of Nature's workmanship that ever crowned a poetic Landskip; those visionary Bards excepted who hold commerce with aerial Beings. –

Had CALUMNY and VILLAINY taken my walk, they had, at that moment sworn eternal peace with such an Object. –

What an hour of inspiration for a Poet! It would have raised plain, dull, historic Prose to Metaphor and Measure!

The inclosed song was the work of my return home: and perhaps but poorly answers what might have been expected from such a scene. – I am going to print a second Edition of my Poems, but cannot insert these verses without your permission. –

> *I have the honor to be,*
> *Madam,*
> *Your most obedient & very humble servant,*
> *Robert Burns*

THE BONIE LASS O' BALLOCHMYLE

'Twas even. The dewy fields were green,
   On every blade the pearls hang;
The zephyrs wanton'd round the bean,
   And bore its fragrant sweets alang;
   In every glen the mavis sang,
All Nature listening seem'd the while,
Except where greenwood echoes rang,
   Amang the braes o' Ballochmyle.

With careless step I onward stray'd,
   My heart rejoic'd in Nature's joy,
When musing in a lonely glade,
   A maiden fair I chanc'd to spy:
Her look was like the morning's eye,
   Her hair like Nature's vernal smile;
   The lilie's hue and roses die
Bespoke the Lass o' Ballochmyle.

Fair is the morn in flow'ry May
And sweet the night in autumn mild;
When roving thro' the garden gay,
   Or wand'ring in the lonely wild;
But Woman, Nature's darling child!
There all her charms she does compile,
Even there her other works are foil'd,
   By th' bonie Lass o' Ballochmyle.

O! had she been a country maid,
And I the happy country swain,
Tho' shelter'd in the lowest shed
That ever rose on Scotland's plain!
Thro' weary winter's wind and rain,
With joy, with rapture, I would toil;
And nightly to my bosom strain
The bonie Lass o' Ballochmyle!

Then pride might climb the slipp'ry steep,
Where fame and honours lofty shine;
And thirst of gold might tempt the deep,
Or downward seek the Indian mine;
Give me the cot below the pine,
To tend the flocks or till the soil;
And every day have joys divine
With the bonie Lass o' Ballochmyle.

Mary Campbell

In the year 1786 Burns was still bitterly disposed towards Jean Armour when he started his affair with Mary Campbell. Jean's father had dispatched her off to live with a distant relative until her pregnancy was over which Burns continued to believe was an act of treachery on the part of Jean. Mary Campbell had originally been employed as a nurse-maid in the house of Burns' friend, Gavin Hamilton, but latterly was a dairy-maid at a nearby farm.

Reports of her character are varied in the extreme, but it appears that the majority of Burns' friends regarded Mary as being beneath him and tried to dissuade the Bard from continuing with the relationship.

Burns, however, had other ideas and arranged that he and Mary should leave Scotland and sail to Jamaica together. Jamaica was a favourite refuge in the 18th century for young Scots in trouble.

They were to meet at Greenock after settling their affairs in Scotland, but before this happened, tragedy struck. Mary died, whether of fever or premature childbirth still remains uncertain. Mary's family had no doubt it was the fault of Burns and her father refused to have his name ever spoken of again in his household. Burns was distraught over the death of his Highland Mary and never forgot her.

MY HIGHLAND LASSIE, O

Nae gentle dames tho' ne'er sae fair
  Shall ever be my Muses care;
  Their titles a' are empty show,
  Gi'e me my Highland Lassie, O.

Chorus –
Within the glen sae bushy, O,
Aboon the plain sae rashy, O,
I set me down wi' right gude will
To sing my Highland Lassie, O.

O were yon hills and vallies mine
  Yon palace and yon gardens fine;
  The world then the love should know
  I bear my Highland Lassie, O.

But fickle fortune frowns on me,
  And I maun cross the raging sea;
  But while my crimson currents flow,
  I love my Highland Lassie, O.

Altho' thro' foreign climes I range,
I know her heart will never change;
For her bosom burns with honor's glow,
My faithful Highland Lassie, O, –

For her I'll dare the billow's roar;
For her I'll trace a distant shore;
That Indian wealth may lustre throw
Around my Highland Lassie, O, –

She has my heart, she has my hand,
By secret troth and honor's band;
Till the mortal stroke shall lay me low,
I'm thine, my Highland Lassie, O, –

Farewell, the glen sae bushy! O,
Farewell, the plain sae rashy! O,
To other lands I now must go
To sing my Highland Lassie, O.

aboon = above; maun = must; crimson currents = blood

Burns was still very melancholy over the death of Mary Campbell some three years after her death. He sent the following poem to his friend, Mrs Dunlop, asking for her opinion as he considered himself too emotionally involved to judge its merit:

I shall send you a Song I made the other day, of which your opinion, as I am far too much interested in the subject of it to be a Critic in the composition.

He sent another lengthy letter to Mrs Dunlop a few weeks later, again referring to Mary, but also discussing the question of life after death:

Can it be possible that when I resign this frail, feverish being, I shall still find myself in conscious existence! When the last gasp of agony has announced that I am no more to those that knew me & the few who loved me: when the cold, stiffened, unconscious, ghastly corpse is resigned into the earth, to be the prey of unsightly reptiles, & to become in time a trodden clod, shall I yet be warm in life, seeing & seen, enjoying and enjoyed?

It continues:

There should I, with speechless agony of rapture, again recognise my lost, my ever dear MARY, whose bosom was fraught with Truth, Honor, Constancy & LOVE. Jesus Christ, thou amiablest of characters, I trust thou art no Imposter, & that thy revelation of blissful scenes of existence beyond death and the grave, is not one of the many impositions which time after time have been palmed on credulous mankind ...

TO MARY IN HEAVEN

Thou lingering Star with lessening ray
That lovest to greet the early morn,
Again thou usherest in the day
My Mary from my Soul was torn –
O Mary! dear, departed Shade!
Where is thy place of blissful rest?
Seest thou thy Lover lowly laid?
Hearest thou the groans that rend his breast?

That sacred hour can I forget,
Can I forget the hallowed grove,
Where by the winding Ayr we met,
To live one day of Parting Love?
Eternity can not efface
Those records dear of transports past!
Thy image at our last embrace,
Ah, little thought we 'twas our last!

Ayr, gurgling, kissed his pebbled shore,
O'er hung with wild-woods, thick'ning, green;
The fragrant birch, and hawthorn hoar,
'Twined, am'rous, round the raptured scene;
The flow'rs sprang wanton to be prest,
The birds sang love on ev'ry spray;
Till, too, too soon the glowing west
Proclaim'd the speed of winged day –

Still o'er these scenes my mem'ry wakes,
And fondly broods with miser-care;
Time but th' impression stronger makes,
As streams their channels deeper wear;
My Mary, dear, departed Shade!
Where is thy place of blissful rest?
Seest thou thy Lover lowly laid?
Hearest thou the groans that rend his breast?

The memory of Mary Campbell was indeed inscribed deep in the heart of Robert Burns, for in spite of a stormy and turbulent period in his life, his memory of her was still fresh as he penned the following words in her memory six years after her tragic death. He wrote in a letter to George Thomson:

In my early years, when I was thinking of going to the West Indies, I took the following farewell of a dear girl … You must know that all my early love-songs were the breathing of ardent Passion; & tho' it might have been easy in after-times to have given them a polish, yet that polish to me, whose they were, & who perhaps alone cared for them, would have defaced the legend of my heart which was so faithfully inscribed on them, Their uncouth simplicity was, as they say of wines, their RACE.

WILL YE GO TO THE INDIES, MY MARY?

Will ye go to the Indies, my Mary,
And leave auld Scotia's shore?
Will ye go to the Indies, my Mary,
Across th' Atlantic roar?

O sweet grows the lime and the orange
And the apples on the pine;
But a' the charms o' the Indies
Can never equal thine.

I hae sworn by the Heavens to my Mary,
I hae sworn by the Heavens to be true;
And sae may the Heavens forget me,
When I forget my vow!

O plight me your faith, my Mary,
And plight me your lily-white hand;
O plight me your faith, my Mary,
Before I leave Scotia's strand.

We hae plighted our troth, my Mary,
In mutual affection to join;
And curst be the cause that shall part us,
The hour and the moment o' time!!!

Shortly afterwards he wrote again to Thomson with the following song:

The Subject of the Song is one of the most interesting passages of my youthful days; & I own that I would be much flattered to see the verses set to an Air which would insure celebrity. Perhaps, after all, 'tis the still glowing prejudice of my heart, that throws a borrowed luster over the merits of the Composition.

HIGHLAND MARY

Ye banks, and braes, and streams around,
The castle o' Montgomerie,
Green be your woods, and fair your flowers,
Your waters never drumlie!
There Simmer first unfauld her robes,
And there the longest tarry!
For there I took the last fareweel,
O my sweet Highland Mary!

How sweetly bloom'd the gay, green birk,
How rich the hawthorn's blossom,
As underneath their fragrant shade,
I clasp'd her to my bosom!
The golden hours on angel's wings
Flew o'er me and my dearie;
For dear to me as light and life
Was my sweet Highland Mary.

Wi' mony a vow and lock'd embrace
Our parting was fu' tender;
And pledging aft to meet again,
We tore oursels asunder,
But O! fell Death's untimely frost,
That nipt my flower sae early!
Now green's the sod, and cauld's the clay,
That wraps my Highland Mary!

O, pale, pale now those rosy lips
I aft hae kissed sae fondly;
And clos'd for ay, the sparkling glance
That dwalt on me sae kindly;
And mould'ring now in silent dust
That heart that lo'ed me dearly!
But still within my bosom's core
Shall live my Highland Mary.

drumlie = muddy; birk = birch

Susan Logan

There was no romantic connection between Burns and Susan Logan. She was merely a friend to whom he had sent a copy of Beattie's poems and had enclosed the following verses as a New Year gift.

TO MISS LOGAN

Again the silent wheels of time
Their annual round have driv'n,
And you, tho' scarce in maiden prime,
Are so much nearer Heav'n.

No gifts have I from Indian coasts
The infant year to hail;
I send you more than India boasts
In Edwin's simple tale,

Our Sex, with guile and faithless love
Is charg'd, perhaps too true;
But may, dear Maid, each Lover prove
An Edwin still to you.

Mrs Elizabeth Scott

Burns had received a wonderful, witty poem written by Mrs Elizabeth Scott of Wauchope Hall, by Jedburgh. She had read the Kilmarnock Edition and was obviously extremely impressed by it. Her poem was written in the Auld Scots manner and in it she questions whether Burns was really a ploughman as she knew of no ploughman who could quote from the Greek Classics, or who would be able to make jokes about the country's political leaders. In fact she feels that such knowledge could only be gained through close association with such people.

She tells him that she would much rather spend an evening listening to him than in entertaining dull aristocrats. If she only knew where he lived she would be delighted to send him a plaid in the marled style.

Burns' answer to her is interesting as he recalls his days working with Nelly Kilpatrick and tells how she was his inspiration to write songs and poems, but how he was too shy and inexperienced to tell her how much he liked her.

Burns was very impressed by Mrs Scott, as the opening lines of a letter he sent her show, and he made a point of visiting Wauchope Hall on his Border tour in 1787:

I do not think I ever met with any letter that was more entertaining than the agreeable one you wrote on the 20th; the circumstances in it are very cleverly placed, and yet seem to rise naturally throughout it, and tho' keenly satirical have not a hint of the indelicate.

TO THE GUIDWIFE OF WAUCHOPE HALL
THE ANSWER

I mind it weel in early date,
When I was beardless, young and blate;
An' first cou'd thresh the barn,
Or haud a yoking at the pleugh,
An' tho' fu' foughten sair enough,
Yet unco proud to learn.
When first amang the yellow corn
A man I reckon'd was;
An' with the lave ilk merry morn
Could rank my rig and lass;
Still shearing and clearing
The tither mindfu' raw;
With claivers and haivers
Wearing the time awa';

Ev'n then a wish (I mind its power)
A wish that to my latest hour
Shall strongly heave my breast;

45

That I for poor auld Scotland's sake
Some useful plan, or book could make,
Or sing a sang at least.
The rough burr-thistle spreading wide
Amang the bearded bear,
I turn'd my weeding heuk aside,
An' spar'd the symbol dear.
No nation, no station
My envy e'er could raise;
A Scot still, but blot still,
I knew no higher praise.

But still the elements o' sang
In formless jumble, right an' wrang,
Wild floated in my brain;
Till on that hairst I said before,
My partner in the merry core,
She rous'd the forming strain.
I see her yet, the sonsy quean,
That lighted up my jingle;
Her pauky smile, her kittle een,
That gar't my heart-strings tingle.
So tiched, bewitched,
I rav'd ay to myself;
But bashing and dashing,
I kend na how to tell.

Hale to the sex, ilk guid chiel says,
Wi' merry dance in winter-days,
An' we to share in common;
The gust o' joy, the balm of woe,
The saul o' life, the heav'n below,
Is rapture-giving woman.
Ye surly sumphs who hate the name,
Be mindful' o' your mither;
She, honest woman, may think shame
That ye're connected with her,
Ye're wae men, ye're nae men,
That slight the lovely dears;
To shame ye, disclaim ye,
Ilk honest birkie swears.

For you, na bred to barn and byre,
Wha sweetly tune the Scottish lyre,
Thanks to you for your line.
The marled plaid ye kindly spare,
By me should gratefully be ware;
'Twad please me to the Nine.
I'd be mair vauntie o' my hap,
Douse hingin o'er my curple,
Than ony ermine ever lap,
Or proud imperial purple.
Farewell then, lang hale then,
An' plenty be your fa';
May losses and crosses
Ne'er at your hallan ca'.

R. Burns.
March 1787

mind it weel = remember it well; blate = shy; haud a yoking = do a day's work; an' tho' fu' foughten
sair enough = and though tired and sore; lave = others; ilk = each; tither = other; claivers and haivers
= nonsense and chatter; bearded bear = barley; heuk = hook; hairst = harvest; core = crowd, sonsy
quean = good-natured girl; kittle een = shrewd eyes; gar't = made; saul = soul; sumphs = boorish
people; birkie = fellow

Isabella MacLeod

Burns had probably met this young lady and her family through his friend, Gavin Hamilton. Her father was Laird of Raasay and was doubtless a man of substance. The first poem appears to indicate that he is thanking her for a gift, but the second one is more of a note of condolence.

TO MISS ISABELLA MACLEOD

The crimson blossom charms the bee,
The summer sun the swallow;
So dear this tuneful gift to me
From lovely Isabella.

Her portrait fair upon my mind
Revolving Time shall mellow;
And Mem'ry's latest effort find
The lovely Isabella.

No Bard or Lover's rapture this,
In fancies vain and shallow;
She is, so come my soul to bliss;
The lovely Isabella.

However, the MacLeod family suffered some tragedies and Burns composed another poem to Isabella in which he alludes to them.
He wrote:

I composed these verses on Miss Isabella MacLeod of Raza, alluding to her feelings on the death of her sister, and the still more melancholy death of her sister's husband, the late Earl of Loudon, who shot himself out of sheer heart-break at some mortification he suffered, owing to the deranged state of his finances.

RAVING WINDS AROUND HER BLOWING

Raving winds around her blowing,
Yellow leaves the woodlands strowing,
By a river hoarsely roaring
Isabella stray'd deploring.
Farewell, hours that late did measure
Sunshine days of joy and pleasure;
Hail thou gloomy night of sorrow,
Cheerless night that knows no morrow.

O'er the Past too fondly wandering,
On the hopeless Future pondering;
Chilly Grief my life-blood freezes,
Fell Despair my fancy seizes.
Life, thou soul of every blessing,
Load to Misery most distressing,
Gladly how I would resign thee,
And to dark Oblivion join thee!

Isabella's brother also died at a very early age and his death was noted by Burns.

ON READING, IN A NEWSPAPER, THE DEATH OF JOHN MACLEOD, ESQ.
BROTHER TO A YOUNG LADY, A PARTICULAR FRIEND OF THE AUTHOR'S

Sad thy tale, thou idle page,
And rueful thy alarms;
Death tears the brother of her love
From Isabella's arms.

Sweetly deckt with pearly dew
The morning rose may blow;
But cold successive noontide blasts
May lay its beauties low.

Fair on Isabella's morn
The sun propitious smil'd;
But, long ere noon, succeeding clouds
Succeeding hopes beguil'd.

Fate oft tears the bosom chords
That Nature finest strung;
So Isabella's heart was form'd,
And so that heart was wrung.

Dread Omnipotence, alone,
Can heal the wound He gave;
Can point the brimful grief-worn eyes
To scenes beyond the grave.

Virtues blossoms there shall blow,
And fear no withering blast;
There Isabella's spotless worth
Shall happy be at last.

Rachel Ainslie

While on his Border tour Robert and his friend, Robert Ainslie, stayed at the house of Ainslie's family where Burns met Ainslie's sister, Rachel.

He recorded in his journal:

Her person a little embonpoint, but handsome; her face, particularly her eyes, full of sweetness and good humour – she unites three qualities rarely to be found together – keen, solid penetration; sly, witty observation and remark; and the gentlest, most unaffected female modesty.

Burns attended church with the family and noticed Rachel becoming slightly distressed as the preacher ranted on about what would become of sinners in the next world. He scribbled down a few lines and presented them to her.

LINES TO MISS AINSLIE

Fair maid, you need not take the hint,
Nor idle texts pursue;
'Twas guilty sinners that he meant,
Not Angels such as you!

Jane Ferrier

By the year 1787 Robert Burns had become the darling of Edinburgh's wealthy society and was welcomed into drawing rooms all over the city. Among his new-found circle of friends and social acquaintances was a young and beautiful woman named Jane Ferrier.

Her father was a leading light in the city's legal profession and was a man of substance. He had built a house in George Street, which was to become one of the city's most prosperous thoroughfares.

Burns appears to have relished rubbing shoulders with such people, but one must wonder if too much exposure to the life of the rich in Edinburgh may have been the catalyst for his world-famous *A Man's a Man For a' That* in which he mocks those with titles and scorns anyone who abuses his wealth at the expense of the poor.

Jane Ferrier had requested a copy of a poem from the Bard which he sent along with this short and flattering poem:

TO MISS FERRIER

Nae Heathen name shall I prefix,
Frae Pindus or Parnassus;
Auld Reekie dings them a' to sticks
For rhyme inspiring Lasses.

Jove's tunefu' Dochters, three times three
Made Homer deep their debtor;
But gi'en the body half an e'e,
Nine Ferriers wad done better.

Last day my mind was in a bog,
Down George's Street I stoited;
A creeping, cauld prosaic fog
My very senses doited.

Do what I dought to set her free,
My Muse lay in the mire;
You turn'd a neuk – I saw your e'e
She took the wing like fire.

The mournfu' Sang I here inclose,
In GRATITUDE I send you;
And pray in rhyme, sincere as prose,
A' GUID THINGS MAY ATTEND YOU.

Robt.Burns
St James Square
Saturday even

frae = from; Auld Reekie = Edinburgh; dings them a' to sticks = knocks down; dochters = daughters; stoited = wandered; cauld = cold; doited = dulled; saul = soul; neuk = corner

Anon

The subject of these verses has remained a mystery all these years. She   believed to be someone who Burns met on his travels as he rode to and from Edinburgh, but he had no intention of giving anything away when he wrote:

The song alludes to part of my private history, which it is of no consequence to the world to know.

YON WILD MOSSY MOUNTAINS

Yon wild, mossy mountains sae lofty and wide,
That nurse in their bosoms the youth o' the Clyde;
Where the grouse lead their coveys thro' the heather to feed,
And the shepherd tents his flock as he pipes on his reed.

Not Gowrie's rich valley, nor Forth's sunny shores,
To me hae the charm o' yon wild, mossy moors;
For there by a lanely, sequestered stream,
Resides a sweet Lassie, my thoughts and my dream. –

Amang thae wild mountains shall still be my path,
Ilk stream foaming down in its ain green, narrow strath;
For there, wi' my Lassie, the day-long I rove,
While o'er us, unheeded, flee the swift hours o' Love. –

She is not the fairest, altho' she is fair;
O' nice education but sma' is her skair;
Her parentage humble as humble can be;
But I lo'e the dear Lassie because she lo'es me. –

To Beauty what man but maun yield him a prize,
In her armour of glances, and blushes, and sighs;
And when Wit and Refinement has polish'd her darts,
They dazzle our een, as they flie to our hearts. –

But Kindness, sweet Kindness, in the fond-sparkling e'e,
Has lustre outshining the diamond to me;
And the heart-beating love as I'm clasped in her arms,
O, these are my Lassie's all-conquering charms. –

Lady Onlie

This is probably an old folk-song collected by Burns on his Highland tour in the late summer of 1787 and revised by him.

A' the lads o' Thornie-bank
When they gae to the shore o' Bucky,
They'll step in an' tak a pint
Wi' Lady Onlie, honest lucky.

Chorus
Ladie Onlie, honest lucky,
Brews gude ale at shore o' Bucky;
I wish her sale for her gude ale,
The best on a' the shore o' Bucky.

Her house sae bien, her curch sae clean,
I wat she is a dainty Chuckie!
And cheary blinks the ingle-gleede
O' Lady Onlie, honest lucky.

curch = scarf, handkerchief; dainty Chuckie = old dear; ingle-gleede = blazing fire

Euphemia Murray

Robert Burns was by now enjoying the hospitality of the aristocracy of Scotland as he travelled the country. His fame as Scotland's Bard made him a desirable house guest in their castles and mansions.

On this occasion he was in the residence of Sir William Murray of Ochtertyre where he met Sir William's cousin, 18-year-old Euphemia Murray, whose beauty had caused her to be known as The Flower of Strathmore.

Burns wrote:

I composed these verses while I stayed at Ochtertyre with Sir Wm Murray. The lady, who was at Ochtertyre at the same time, was the well-known toast, Miss Euphemia Murray of Lentrose, who was called, and very justly, The Flower of Strathmore.

Unfortunately, he chose to write the song to the tune *Andrew and his Cutty Gun*, which was an old bawdy song with direct reference to a phallic symbol, and Euphemia was not amused even though the song was highly complimentary to her.

BLYTHE, BLYTHE AND MERRY WAS SHE

By Ochtertyre grows the aik,
On Yarrow banks the birken shaw;
But Phemie was a bonier lass
Than braes o' Yarrow ever saw.

Chorus
Blythe, blythe and merry was she,
Blythe was she but and ben;
Blythe by the banks of Ern,
And blythe in Glenturit glen.

Her looks were like a flower in May,
Her smile was like a simmer morn,
She tripped by the banks of Ern
As light as a bird upon a thorn.

Her bonie face it was as meek
As ony lamb upon a lea;
The evening sun was ne'er sae sweet
As was the blink o' Phemie's e'e.

The Highland hills I've wander'd wide
And o'er the lawlands I hae been;
But Phemie was the blithest lass
That ever trod the dewy green.

aik = oak; birken shaw = birch wood

Margaret Chalmers

This particular Peggy was Margaret Chalmers, a cousin of Burns' friend, Gavin Hamilton, and a good friend of Hamilton's sister, Charlotte. Burns was captivated by Margaret Chalmers and wrote screeds of letters to her, continuing long after she had married and his own life had moved on. She confided to someone in later years that Burns had proposed marriage to her but that she had refused his offer. This refusal did not deter the Bard from considering her to be a true and trusted friend to whom he could reveal his innermost thoughts in his letters to her. Although some of these letters have survived, it appears that her cousin Charlotte considered them inappropriate and threw most of them onto the hearth. Burns sent a copy of the first song to Margaret who was concerned what people might think of her, and in a letter of reassurance he wrote:

The poetic compliments I pay cannot be misunderstood. They are neither of them so particular as to point you out to the world at large; and the circle of your acquaintances will allow all I have said. Besides I have complimented you chiefly, almost solely on your mental charms. Shall I be plain with you? I will; so look to it. Personal attractions, madam, you have much above par; wit, understanding and worth, you possess in the first class. This is a cursed flat way of telling you these truths, but let me hear no more of your sheepish timidity.

MY PEGGY'S FACE

My Peggy's face, my Peggy's form,
The frost of hermit age might warm;
My Peggy's worth, my Peggy's mind,
Might charm the first of human kind.
I love my Peggy's angel air,
Her face so truly heav'nly fair,
Her native grace so void of art,
But I adore my Peggy's heart.

The lily's hue, the roses die,
The kindling lustre of an eye;
Who but owns their magic sway,
Who but knows they all decay!
The tender thrill, the pitying tear,
The generous purpose nobly dear,
The gentle look that Rage disarms,
These are all Immortal charms.

His feelings towards Peggy are transparently clear in an earlier letter in which he writes:

I know you will laugh at it, when I tell you that your Piano and you together have play'd the deuce somehow about my heart ... I was once a zealous Devotee to your Sex, but you know the black story at home. My breast has been widowed these many months, and I thought myself proof against the fascinating witchcraft; but I am afraid you will 'feelingly convince me what I am' – I say I am afraid, because I am not sure what is the matter with me. – I have one miserable bad symptom, when you whisper, or look kindly to another, it gives me a draught of damnation ...

This is the second song sent by Burns to Peggy Chalmers:

WHERE BRAVING ANGRY WINTER'S STORMS

Where braving angry Winter's storms
The lofty Ochels rise,
Far in their shade, my Peggy's charms
First blest my wondering eyes.

As one who by some savage stream
A lonely gem surveys,
Astonish'd doubly marks it beam
With art's most polish'd blaze.

Blest be the wild, sequester'd glade
And blest the day and hour,
Where Peggy's charms I first survey'd,
When first I felt their pow'r.

The tyrant Death with grim controul
May seize my fleeting breath,
But tearing Peggy from my soul
Must be a stronger death.

Charlotte Hamilton

This time the subject of the poem is Charlotte Hamilton and Burns had a few words to say about her. However, could it be that this was a case of Burns attempting to ingratiate himself with Charlotte in the hope that this might help him in his pursuit of her cousin?

These verses were composed on a charming girl, a Miss Charlotte Hamilton, who is now married to Jas McKitrick Adair, Esquire, Physician. She is sister to my worthy friend, Gavin Hamilton, of Mauchline; and was born on the banks of Ayr, but was, at the time I wrote these lines, residing at Herveyston, in Clackmannan Shire, on the romantic banks of the river Devon.

And in another letter to Gavin Hamilton:

Of Charlotte I cannot speak in common terms of admiration; she is not only beautiful, but lovely. – Her form is elegant; her features not regular but they have the smile of Sweetness and the settled complacency of good nature in the highest degree …

THE BANKS OF THE DEVON

How pleasant the banks of the clear-winding Devon,
With green-spreading bushes, and flowers blooming fair!
But the boniest flower on the banks of the Devon
Was once a sweet bud on the braes of the Ayr.
Mild be the sun on this sweet-blushing Flower,
In the gay, rosy morn as it bathes in the dew;
And gentle the fall of the soft, vernal shower,
That steals on the evening each leaf to renew!

O spare the dear blossom, ye orient breezes,
With chill, hoary wing as ye usher the dawn!
And far be thou distant, thou reptile that seizes
The verdure and pride of the garden or lawn!
Let Bourbon exult in his gay, gilded Lilies,
And England triumphant display her proud Rose,
A fairer than either adores the green vallies
Where Devon, sweet Devon meandering flows. –

Clementina Walkinshaw

This song was written about the daughter of Prince Charles Edward and his mistress, Clementina Walkinshaw, who was eventually to become the Countess of Albany.

THE BONIE LASS OF ALBANIE

My heart is wae and unco wae,
To think upon the raging sea,
That roars between her gardens green,
And the bonie lass of Albanie.

This lovely maid of noble blood,
That ruled Albion's kingdoms three;
But Oh, Alas! for her bonie face!
They hae wrang'd the lass of Albanie!

In the rolling tide of spreading Clyde
There sits an isle of high degree;
And a town of fame whose princely name
Should grace the lass of Albanie.

But there is a youth, a witless youth,
That fills the place where she should be,
We'll send him to his native shore,
And bring our ain sweet Albanie.

Alas the day, and woe the day,
A false Usurper wan the gree
That now commands the towers and lands
The royal right of Albanie.

We'll daily pray, we'll nightly pray,
On bended knee most ferventlie,
That the time may come, with pipes and drum,
We'll welcome home fair Albanie.

wae = woe; Albion's kingdom's three = England, Scotland and Ireland; an isle of high degree = isle of Bute; town of fame = Rothesay; witless youth = Prince George, later King George IV

Nancy McLehose (Clarinda)

Robert Burns' relationship with Nancy McLehose, known to the world as Clarinda, is one of the great romantic tales of all time and has been the subject of many dissertations over the years. It is a story that merits a book all of its own, and the sheer volume of letters that passed between them makes it impossible to do it full justice in this volume.

Agnes Craig, better known as Nancy, was born in Glasgow and had been given the benefit of a good education, unusual for women in those days. She was an attractive young lady who caught the eye of a young Glasgow lawyer named James McLehose, who, on discovering that Nancy was about to travel to Edinburgh by coach, booked all the other seats in the carriage! His ploy worked and during the 10 hours spent in her company on the journey, he persuaded her to become his wife.

But four children later and too many brutal beatings at his hands saw the marriage founder, and James set off for the West Indies leaving Nancy behind. She took up residence in Edinburgh where she was largely dependent upon charitable aid and assistance from relatives. However, she was an unusually literary young lady and was readily accepted within Edinburgh's drawing-room society.

Nancy certainly does not appear to have been a shy, retiring young woman, for she had heard of the young poet who was rapidly becoming the darling of Edinburgh and set out to meet him by contriving an invitation to a house where she knew he would also be invited. This meeting was a great success and immediately Robert Burns was smitten by the attractive young woman. When she then displayed a wide knowledge of poetry and literature, it was the start of a relationship that was to last for almost seven years and which would generate hundreds of letters between the pair.

It was also the most frustrating relationship ever experienced by Burns, for Nancy was still a married woman and had no intention of allowing the poet the sort of intimacy that he normally found his women friends willing to engage in.

However, he started out with high hopes and almost immediately after their first meeting wrote:

I can say with truth, Madam, that I never met with a person in my life whom I more anxiously wished to meet again than yourself. Tonight I was to have had that very great pleasure ... I was so intoxicated with the idea ... but an unlucky fall from a coach has so bruised one of my knees that I can't stir my leg off the cushion. So if I don't see you again, I shall not rest in my grave for chagrin ... I was vexed to the soul that I had not seen you sooner; I determined to cultivate your friendship with the enthusiasm of Religion; but thus Fortune ever served me ... I cannot bear the idea of leaving Edinburgh without seeing you ... I know not how to account for I ... I am strangely taken with some people, nor am I often mistaken. You are a stranger to me; but I am an odd being; some yet unnamed feelings; things not principles, but better than whims carry me farther than boasted reason ever did a Philosopher. –
Farewell! Every happiness be yours!

Robt Burns

So it began. Nancy answered his letters almost immediately, including with them her own poetic contributions, until she realised that she was putting herself into a compromising situation by signing them, so to protect their anonymity she suggested that she would become Clarinda and he Sylvander, an idea that Burns greeted with enthusiasm.

Time is too short for ceremonies – I swear solemnly (in all the tenor of my former oath) to remember you in all the pride and warmth of friendship until – I cease to be!
Tomorrow and every day till I see you, you shall hear from me. –

ANSWER TO CLARINDA

When first you saw Clarinda's charms
What raptures in your bosom grew!
Her heart was shut to love's alarms,
But then – you'd nothing else to do.

Apollo oft had lent his harp,
But now 'twas strung from Cupid's bow;
You sung, it reach'd Clarinda's heart,
She wish'd – you'd nothing else to do.

Fair Venus smil'd, Minerva frown'd
Cupid observ'd, the arrow flew;
Indifference (ere a week went round)
Shew'd – you'd nothing else to do.

The correspondence between them was by now a daily occurrence and the letters were getting longer and longer as each of them vied to produce poetry.
In one lengthy epistle dated 4 January 1788 Burns wrote:

Your last verses to me have so delighted me, that I have got an excellent old Scots air that suits the measure, and you shall see them in print in the Scots Musical Museum, *a work publishing by a friend of mine in this town. I want four stanzas; you gave me but three, and one alluded to an expression in my former letter, so I have taken your first two verses with a slight alteration in the second, and have added a third, but you must help me to a fourth. Here they are; the latter half of the first stanza would have been worthy of Sappho; I am in raptures with it ...*

Talk not of Love, it gives me pain,
For love has been my foe;
He bound me with an iron chain,
And sunk me deep in woe. –

In another poem to Clarinda, answering one of her letters, he appears to be reluctantly acknowledging her declaration that this would indeed be a platonic friendship and that he would not be allowed to do 'the deed' with Clarinda.

When dear Clarinda, matchless fair,
First struck Sylvander's raptur'd view,
He gaz'd, he listen'd to despair,
Alas! 'twas all he dar'd to do.

Love, from Clarinda's heavenly eyes,
Transfix'd his bosom thro' and thro';
But still in Friendship's guarded guise,
Far more the demon fear'd to do.

That heart, already more than lost,
The imp beleaguer'd all perdue;
For frowning Honor kept his post,
To meet that frown he shrunk to do.

His pangs the Bard refus'd to own,
Tho' half he wish'd Clarinda knew;
But Anguish wrung th' unweeting groan –
Who blames what frantic Pain must do?

That heart, where motley follies blend,
Was sternly still to Honor true;
To prove Clarinda's fondest friend,
Was what a Lover sure might do.

The Muse his ready quill employ'd,
No dearer bliss he could pursue;
That bliss Clarinda cold deny'd –
'Send word by Charles how you do!'

The chill behest disarm'd his muse,
Till Passion all impatient grew;
He wrote, and hinted for excuse,
'Twas 'cause he'd nothing else to do.'

But by these hopes I have above!
And by these faults I dearly rue!
The deed, that boldest mark of love,
For thee that deed I dare to do!

O, would the Fates but name the price,
Would bless me with your charms and you!
With frantic joy I'd pay it thrice,
If human art or power could do!

Then take, Clarinda, friendship's hand,
(Friendship, at least, I may avow;)
And lay no more your chill command,
I'll write, whatever I've to do.

Sylvander

Although Burns was never able to seduce Clarinda, this certainly did not prevent him from sleeping with other women. As he pursued Clarinda through the medium of letters, poems and songs, he got a young servant girl by the name of Jenny Clow pregnant, resulting in the birth of a son.

But even this failed to slow Burns down in his pursuit of Clarinda, and so it continued – more and more letters, more and more poems.

REVISION FOR CLARINDA

Go on, sweet bird, and soothe my care,
Thy tuneful notes will hush Despair;
Thy plaintiff warblings, void of art
Thrill sweetly thro' my aching heart.
Now chuse thy mate, and fondly love,
And all the charming transports prove;
While I a lovelorn exile live,
Nor transport or receive or give.

For thee is laughing Nature gay;
For thee she pours the vernal day;
For me in vain is Nature drest,
While joy's a stranger to my breast!
These sweet emotions all enjoy;
Let love and song the hours enjoy;
Go on, sweet bird, and soothe my care;
Thy tuneful notes will hush Despair.

In another extract from a letter it is obvious that Clarinda has passed by his lodgings but failed to see him:

I could almost have thrown myself over for very vexation. Why didn't you look higher? It has spoilt my peace for this day. To be so near my charming Clarinda; to miss her look when it was searching for me – I am sure the soul is capable of disease, for mine has convulsed into an inflamatory fever.

Some 10 days and several letters later in another letter written at 10:30pm:

What luxury of bliss I was enjoying this time yesternight! My ever-dearest Clarinda, you have stolen away my soul but you have refined, you have exalted it; you have given it a stronger sense of Virtue, and a stronger relish for Piety – Clarinda, first of your Sex, if ever I am the veriest wretch on earth to forget you; if ever your lovely image is effaced from my soul,

> *'May I be lost, no eye to weep my end;*
> *And find no earth that's base enough to bury me!'*

CLARINDA, MISTRESS OF MY SOUL

> Clarinda, mistress of my soul,
> The measur'd time is run!
> The wretch beneath the dreary pole,
> So marks his latest sun.
>
> To what dark cave of frozen night
> Shall poor Sylvander hie;
> Depriv'd of thee, his life and light,
> The Sun of all his joy.
>
> We part – but by these precious drops,
> That fill thy lovely eyes!
> No other light shall guide my steps,
> Till thy bright beams arise.
>
> She, the fair Sun of all her sex,
> Has blest my glorious day;
> And shall a glimmering Planet fix
> My worship to its ray?

The strength of feeling that Burns had for Clarinda was incredible, particularly as so much of their relationship was conducted at a distance. This letter which he sent her on 14 March 1788 reveals how much he cherished her friendship:

I am just now come in, and have read your letter. The first thing I did, was to thank the Divine Disposer of events, that he has had such happiness in store for me as the connexion I have with you. Life, my Clarinda, is a weary, barren path; and woe be to him or her that ventures on it alone! For me, I have my dearest partner of my soul: Clarinda and I will make our pilgrimage together. Wherever I am, I shall constantly let her know how I go on, what I observe in the world around me, and what adventures I meet with. Will it please you, my love, to get, every week, or, at least every fortnight, a packet, two or three sheets, full of remarks, nonsense, news, rhymes, and old songs?

Will you open, with satisfaction and delight, a letter from a man who loves you, who has loved you, and who will love you to death, through death, and forever? Oh Clarinda! what do I owe to Heaven for blessing me with such a piece of exalted excellence as you! I call over your idea, as a miser counts over his treasure! Tell me, were you studious to please me last night? I am sure you did it to transport. How rich I am to have such treasure as you! You know me: you know how to make me happy, and you did it most effectually. God bless you with

> *'Long life, long youth, long pleasure, and a friend!'*

Tomorrow night, according to you own directions, I shall watch the window: 'tis the star that guides me to paradise. The great relish to all is, that Honour, that Innocence, that Religion, are the witnesses and guarantees of our happiness. 'The Lord God knoweth,' and perhaps, 'Israel he shall know,' my love and your merit. Adieu, Clarinda! I am going to remember you in my prayers.

Sylvander

Towards the end of March 1788 Burns was called to be interviewed for a position within the Excise. He sent this letter to his beloved Clarinda along with a pair of wine glasses.

I am just hurrying away to wait on the Great Man, Clarinda, but I have more respect for my own peace and happiness than to set out without waiting on you; for my imagination, like a child's favourite bird, will fondly flutter along with this scrawl till it perch on your bosom. – I thank you for all the happiness you bestowed on me yesterday. – The walk, delightful; the evening, rapture …

> Fair Empress of the Poet's soul,
> And Queen of Poetesses;
> Clarinda, take this little boon,
> This humble pair of Glasses.
>
> And fill them high with generous juice,
> As generous as your mind;
> And pledge me in the generous toast –
> 'The whole of Humankind!'

'To those who love us!' second fill;
But not to those whom we love,
Lest we love those who love not us;
A third – 'to thee and me, Love!'

Long may we live! Long may we love!
And long may we be happy!!!
And may we never want a Glass,
Well charged with generous Nappy!!!!

Now, anyone not familiar with the life of Robert Burns will struggle to understand, or even believe, just what he had done in the month of February before that last poem was written. He had left Edinburgh for a short return trip to Ayrshire where he had reinstated Jean Armour as his wife and bought her a mahogany bed as a present. But before returning to Edinburgh, he sent to Clarinda a most infamous letter that does him no credit whatsoever:

Now for a little news that will certainly please you. I, this morning as I came home, called for a certain woman. I am disgusted with her; I cannot endure her! I, while my heart smote me for the prophanity, tried to compare her with my Clarinda: 'twas setting the expiring glimmer of a farthing taper beside the cloudless glory of the meridian sun. Here was tasteless insipidity, vulgarity of soul, and mercenary fawning; there, polished good sense, heaven-born genius, and the most delicate, the most tender Passion. – I have done with her, and she with me.

If Burns thought that this news would please Clarinda, then she must have been in favour of the idea in the first place, and although the letter sounds absolutely heartless, could it be that he simply wanted Clarinda to feel that she was uppermost in his heart and simply went over the top in his reassurances? Later poems and songs in honour of Jean Armour would certainly display Jean in a very favourable light.

Time and events took their toll on the relationship. Burns could not maintain his correspondence with Clarinda and continue to be a husband to Jean, and the relationship deteriorated between them. An extract from this letter shows a different attitude to the love and passion of earlier letters.

I have received both of your last letters, Madam, & ought & would have answered the first long ago. But on what subject shall I write you? How can you expect a Correspondent should write you, when you declare that you mean to preserve his letters with a view, sooner or later, to expose them on the pillory of derision & the rack of criticism? This is gagging me compleately as to speaking the sentiments of my bosom ...

By 1791 Nancy had realized that any possibility of a life with Burns was never going to happen, so she decided to leave Scotland to attempt a reconciliation with her estranged husband in the West Indies. Although Robert Burns was living with his wife, he was still deeply distressed to hear of Nancy's impending departure.

He sent her the two following songs as a reminder, the second of which is one of the most beautiful love songs ever written:

GLOOMY DECEMBER

Ance mair I hail thee, thou gloomy December
Ance mair I hail thee wi' sorrow and care;
Sad was the parting thou makes me remember,
Parting wi' Nancy, Oh ne'er to meet mair!
Fond lover's parting is sweet, painful pleasure,
Hope beaming mild on the soft parting hour,
But the dire feeling, 'O farewell for ever!'
Anguish unmingl'd and agony pure.

Wild as the winter now tearing the forest,
Till the last leaf o' the summer has flown,
Such is the tempest has shaken my bosom
Till my last hope and last comfort is gone:
Still as I hail thee, thou gloomy December,
Still shall I hail thee wi' sorrow and care;
For sad was the parting thou makes me remember,
Parting wi' Nancy, Oh ne'er to meet mair.

AE FOND KISS

Ae fond kiss and then we sever;
Ae fareweel, and then for ever!
Deep in heart-wrung tears I'll pledge thee,
Warring sighs and groans I'll wage thee.
Who shall say that Fortune grieves him,
While the star of hope she leaves him;
Me, nae chearful twinkle lights me;
Dark despair around benights me.

I'll ne'er blame my partial fancy,
Naething could resist my Nancy;
But to see her, was to love her;
Love but her, and love for ever.

Had we never lov'd sae kindly
Had we never lov'd sae blindly!
Never met – or never parted,
We had ne'er been broken-hearted.

Fare-thee-weel, thou first and fairest!
Fare-thee-weel, thou best and dearest!
Thine be ilka joy and treasure,
Peace, Enjoyment, Love and Pleasure!
Ae fond kiss, and then we sever!
Ae fareweel, alas for ever!
Deep in heart-wrung tears I'll pledge thee,
Warring sighs and groans I'll wage thee.

Burns was at his poetic best when producing songs of sadness. He sent the original of this one to Nancy before she set off for Jamaica.

BEHOLD THE HOUR, THE BOAT ARRIVE

Behold the hour, the boat arrive;
Thou goest, thou darling of my heart,
Severed from thee, can I survive,
But fate has willed, and we must part.
I'll often greet this surging swell,
Yon distant isle will often hail;
E'en here I took the last farewell;
There, latest marked her vanished sail.

Along the solitary shore,
While flitting sea-fowl round me cry,
Across the rolling, dashing roar
I'll west-ward turn my wistful eye:
Happy thou Indian grove, I'll say.
Where now my Nancy's path may be!
While through thy sweets she loves to stray,
O tell me, does she muse on me!

Sadly for Nancy, her trip was in vain. Her husband had taken a West Indian woman as his mistress and had no interest in rekindling his marriage. Nancy returned to Scotland, disconsolate, only to find that her darling Sylvander had also lost interest and had moved on to pastures new. She eventually died in Edinburgh, in a house almost under the shadow of the site that the citizens of Edinburgh were to choose as a memorial to Robert Burns.

On her death, the letters that had been sent from Sylvander were considered to be of no value and only the box in which they were contained was sold.

Anne Stewart

This young lady was Anne Stewart of East Craigs who had jilted her fiancé in favour of an Edinburgh surgeon. Burns wrote to his friend, Mrs Dunlop:

The following is a jeu d'esprit of t'other day, on a despairing Lover carrying me to see his Dulcinea …

ANNA, THY CHARMS

Anna, thy charms my bosom fire,
And waste my soul with care;
But ah! how bootless to admire,
When fated to despair!

Yet in thy presence, lovely Fair,
To hope may be forgiven;
For sure 'twere impious to despair
So much in sight of Heaven.

Jean Armour

Robert Burns may have sent his dreadful letter to Clarinda in an attempt to reassure her that she was the only woman in the world for him, but the reality of his relationship with Jean was somewhat different, as the following two poems, written in compliment to Mrs Burns, testify. In a letter written on 25 May 1788 to his friend, James Johnson in Edinburgh, Burns advises him of his marriage to Jean Armour and writes:

I am so enamoured with a certain girl's twin-bearing merit, that I have given her a legal title to the best blood in my body; and so farewell Rakery!

Jean Armour was reinstated as the wife of Robert Burns and remained so until his death. The pair had already gone through a form of marriage in 1786 when Jean became pregnant, but her parents were furious and wished no part of Robert Burns as their son-in-law.

They sent Jean off to live with an aunt in another part of the country where she gave birth to twins. Burns decided this was an act of treachery on the part of Jean and had the marriage annulled. This was the time he commenced his affair with Mary Campbell. However, when he returned from Edinburgh in 1787, he was treated as a celebrity and the Armours were by then keen to have him marry their daughter. Burns detested them for their hypocrisy. Poor Jean became pregnant once again, and this time her parents were so angry that they threw her out onto the streets in an advanced stage of pregnancy where she was rescued by Burns.

It must be said that his conduct at this point was not that of a tender lover, as he wrote the most disgraceful and boastful letter he ever penned to a friend, Robert Ainslie. Burns tells him in great detail how he had laid Jean on a bed of horse litter and had sexual intercourse with her. Over the years, Jean bore Burns nine children, but it certainly appears that the marriage was not initiated by the love and passion he was so keen to portray as essential in such a partnership.

He described the situation in a letter to his old friend, Peggy Chalmers:

Shortly after my last return to Ayrshire, I married 'my Jean.' This was not in consequence of the attachment of romance perhaps, but I have had a long and much-loved fellow creature's happiness or misery in my determination, and I durst not trifle with so important a deposit. Nor have I cause to resent it. If I have not got polite tattle, modish manners, and fashionable dress, I am not sickened and disgusted with the multiform curse of boarding-school affectation; and I have got the handsomest figure, the sweetest temper, the soundest constitution, and the kindest heart in the country.

I LOVE MY JEAN

Of a' the airts the wind can blaw,
  I dearly like the West;
For there the bonie Lassie lives,
  The lassie I lo'e best.
There wild-woods grow, and rivers row,
  And mony a hill between;
But day and night my fancy's flight
  Is ever wi' my Jean.

I see her in the dewy flowers,
  I see her sweet and fair;
I hear her in the tuneful' birds,
  I hear her charm the air;
There's not a bonie flower, that springs
  By fountain, shaw, or green;
There's not a bonie bird that sings
  But minds me o' my Jean.

O, WERE I ON PARNASSUS HILL

O, were I on Parnassus hill;
  O had I o' Helicon my fill;
That I might catch poetic skill,
  To sing how dear I love thee.
But Nith maun be my Muses well,
My Muse maun be thy bonie sell;
On Corsincon I'll glowr and spell,
  And write how dear I love thee.

Then come sweet Muse, inspire my lay!
For a' the lee-lang simmer's day,
I couldna sing, I couldna say,
  How much, how dear I love thee.
I see thee dancing o'er the green,
Thy waist sae jimpy, thy limbs sae clean,
Thy tempting lips, thy roguish een –
  By Heaven and Earth I love thee.

By night, by day, a-field, at hame,
The thoughts o' thee my breast inflame;
And ay I muse and sing thy name,
I only live to love thee.
Tho' I were doom'd to wander on,
Beyond the sea, beyond the sun,
Till my last, weary sand was run;
Till then – and then I love thee.

Another short and rather melancholy poem from the pen of the Bard. This one is credited with being written about his wife, Jean Armour.

THE NORTHERN LASS

Though cruel fate should bid us part,
Far as the Pole and Line,
Her dear idea around my heart
Should tenderly entwine;

Though mountains rise, and deserts howl,
And oceans roar between;
Yet dearer than my deathless soul
I still would love my Jean. –

IT IS NA, JEAN, THY BONIE FACE

It is na, Jean, thy bonie face,
Nor shape that I admire,
Altho' thy beauty and thy grace
Might weel awauk desire.

Something in ilka part o' thee
To praise, to love, I find,
But dear as is thy form to me,
Still dearer is thy mind.

Nae mair ungen'rous wish I hae,
Nor stronger in my breast,
Than, if I canna make thee sae,
At least to see thee blest.

> Content am I, if Heaven will give
> But happiness to thee:
> An' as wi' thee I'd wish to live,
> For thee I'd bear to die.

Burns' attitude towards his wife is difficult to interpret. He seems to have been genuinely fond of her, but she was not overdone in verse, and even less so in letters. In fact, only four letters from Burns to Jean Armour are recorded compared with around 60 to Nancy McLehose, and the content of the letters to Jean is very, very, different. It is of course possible that he wrote other letters to Jean which have been lost or destroyed, for it could be that the wife would have less need to hold onto letters from her husband than a young woman would from her lover. Only the first letter starts off in a truly loving manner:

Ellisland 12th Sept 1788
My dear Love,
I received your kind letter with a pleasure which no letter but one from you could have given me. I dreamed of you the whole night last; but alas! it will be three weeks yet, ere I can hope for the happiness of seeing you. My harvest is going on. I have some to cut down still, but I put in two stacks today, so I am as tired as a dog.

The letter continues with domestic affairs.
Another, from Edinburgh says simply:

I cannot precisely say when I will leave this town, my dearest friend, but at farthest I think I will be with you on Sunday come eight days, perhaps sooner. I had a horrid journey.

Again, some information about his meeting with his publisher, but no words of passion for Jean. They were continuing to be sent to Clarinda!

In February 1795 Burns was marooned in Ecclefechan by a snowstorm and spent some of his time on the following song. It is unclear exactly who the song is written about as the following extract from a letter to Thomson shows. It could be Jean Armour or Jean Lorimer, or perhaps another unknown female:

I think in slowish time it would make an excellent song. I am highly delighted with it; & if you should think it worthy of your attention, I have a fair Dame in my eye to whom I would consecrate it ...

O, WAT YE WHA'S IN YON TOWN?

Chorus
O. wat ye wha's in yon town
Ye see the e'enin sun upon?
The dearest maid in yon town,
That e'enin sun is shining on!.

Now haply down yon gay green shaw
She wanders by yon spreading tree.
How blest the birds that round her blaw!
Ye catch the glances o' her e'e.

How blest ye birds that round her sing,
And welcome in the blooming year!
And doubly welcome be the Spring,
The season to my Jeanie dear!

The sun blinks blythe in yon town,
Among the broomy braes sae green;
But my delight in yon town,
And dearest pleasure is my Jean.

Without my Love, not a' the charms
O' Paradise could yield my joy;
But gi'e me Jeanie in my arms,
And welcome Lapland's dreary sky.

My cave wad be a lover's bow'r,
Tho' raging winter rent the air;
And she a lovely little flower,
That I wad tent and shelter there.

O sweet is she in yon town,
The sinkin' sun's gane down upon;
A fairer than's in yon town,
His setting beam ne'er shone upon.

If angry fate is sworn my foe,
And suffering I am doom'd to bear;
I careless quit aught else below,
But spare me, spare me Jeanie dear.

For life's dearest blood is warm,
Ae though frae her shall ne'er depart,
And she – as fairest in her form,
She has the truest kindest heart.

shaw = wood; tent = tend

Two months later Burns sent this poem to Thomson, but this time there is no doubt that it was written in compliment to Jean Armour.

THEIR GROVES O' SWEET MYRTLE

Their groves o' sweet myrtle let Foreign Lands reckon,
Where bright-beaming summers exalt the perfume,
Far dearer to me yon lone glen o' green breckan
Wi' the burn stealing under the lang, yellow broom;
Far dearer to me are yon humble broom bowers,
Where the bluebell and gowan lurk, lowly, unseen;
For there, lightly tripping amang the wild flowers,
A listening the linnet, oft wanders my Jean.

Tho' rich is the breeze in their gay, sunny vallies,
And cauld, Caledonia's blast on the wave;
Their sweet-scented woodlands that skirt the proud palace,
What are they? The haunt o' the Tyrant and Slave.
The Slave's spicy forests, and gold-bubbling fountains,
The brave Caledonian views wi' disdain;
He wanders as free as the winds of his mountains,
Save Love's willing fetters, the chains o' his Jean.

Burns had been recommended by his doctor to immerse himself in the freezing waters of the Brow Well on the Solway Firth as a cure for his rapidly deteriorating health. This remedy was directly responsible for truncating the life of the Bard, but he had faith in his doctor and did as he was told. One week before his death, he wrote his final letter to Jean Armour:

14th July 1796

My dearest Love,
I delayed writing until I could tell you what effect sea-bathing was likely to produce. It would be injustice to deny that it has eased my pains, and, I think, has strengthened me, but my appetite is still extremely bad. No flesh nor fish can I swallow; porridge and milk are the only things I can taste. I am very happy to hear, by Miss Jess Lewars, that you are all well. My very best and kindest compliments to her, and to all the children. I will see you on Sunday.
Your affectionate husband;
R.B.

Jean Armour outlived her husband by 38 years, and was unable to attend his funeral as she was giving birth to their son, Maxwell, named after the doctor whose treatment had exacerbated her husband's condition. However, Burns' reputation was such that some 10,000 ordinary and well-to-do Scots managed to make their way to Dumfries to witness the procession and burial in St Michael's Kirkyard of one of Scotland's finest sons.

Helen Irvine

This is a wonderful, true story of love and tragedy. Helen Irvine lived in the village of Kirkconnel, Dumfriesshire in the 16th century. She was being courted by a young man named Adam Fleming when a rival suitor happened upon them. In a fit of jealousy, the rival took his pistol and fired at Adam, but Helen leapt in front of him and was fatally wounded by the bullet. Adam drew his sword and slew the assassin on the spot, hacking his body into pieces with maddened fury. Then realising the seriousness of his situation, fled the scene and eventually ended up in Spain where he served for many years in the army. He eventually returned to Scotland to mourn beside the grave of his beloved Helen, and on his death was buried beside her.

WHERE HELEN LIES

O that I were where Helen lies,
Night and day on me she cries;
O that I were where Helen lies
In fair Kirkconnel lee. –

O Helen fair beyond compare,
A ringlet of thy flowing hair,
I'll wear it still for ever mair
Until the day I die.

Curs'd be the hand that shot the shot,
And curs'd the gun that gave the crack!
Into my arms bird Helen lap,
And died for sake o' me!

O think no ye my heart was sair;
My Love fell down and spake nae mair;
There did she swoon wi' meikle care
On fair Kirkconnel lee.

I lighted down, my sword did draw,
I cutted him in pieces sma';
I cutted him in pieces sma'
On fair Kirconnel lee.

O Helen chaste, thou were modest,
If I were with thee I were blest
Where thou lies low and takes thy rest
On fair Kirkconnel lee.

I wish my grave was growing green,
A winding sheet put o'er my e'en,
And I in Helen's arms lying
In fair Kirkconnel lee!

I wish I were where Helen lies!
Night and day on me she cries;
O that I were where Helen lies
On fair Kirkconnel lee.

Jeany Cruikshank

Burns lodged with the Cruikshanks at St James Square, Edinburgh, and Jeany was about 12 years old when he composed these lines in her honour. He was particularly taken by her extraordinary musical talents and loved to hear her sing.

This song I composed on Miss Jeany Cruikshank, only child of my worthy friend, Mr Wm Cruikshank of the High School, Edinr …

A ROSEBUD BY MY EARLY WALK

A rosebud by my early walk,
Adown a corn-enclosed bawk,
Sae gently bent its thorny stalk
All on a dewy morning.

Ere twice the shades o' dawn are fled,
In a' its crimson glory spread,
And drooping rich the dewy head,
It scents the early morning.

Within the bush her covert nest
A little linnet fondly prest,
The dew sat chilly on her breast
Sae early in the morning.

She soon shall see her tender brood
The pride, the pleasure o' the wood,
Amang the fresh green leaves bedew'd,
Awauk the early morning.

So thou, dear bird, young Jenny fair,
On trembling string or vocal air,
Shalt sweetly pay the tender care
That tents thy early morning.

So thou sweet Rosebud, young and gay,
Shalt beauteous blaze upon the day,
And bless the Parent's evening ray
That watch'd thy early morning.

He wrote another poem to Jeany that he presented to her at a later date.

TO MISS CRUIKSHANK,
A VERY YOUNG LADY

Beauteous rose-bud, young and gay,
Blooming on thy early May,
Never may'st thou, lovely Flower,
Chilly shrink in sleety shower!
Never Boreas' hoary path,
Never Eurus' pois'nous breath,
Never baleful stellar lights,
Taint thee with untimely blights!
Never, never reptile thief
Riot on thy virgin leaf!
Nor even Sol too fiercely view
Thy bosom blushing still with dew!

May'st thou long, sweet crimson gem,
Richly deck thy native stem;
Till some evening, sober, calm,
Dropping dews, and breathing balm,
While all around the woodland rings,
And every bird thy requiem sings;
Thou amidst the dirgeful sound,
Shed thy dying honours round,
And resign to Parent Earth
The loveliest form she e'er gave birth.

Peggy Alison

Although the name Peggy Alison appears in the song, historians are uncertain to whom this song was really dedicated. Some put it down to Alison Begbie, while others consider Mary Campbell as being more likely.

AN' I'LL KISS THEE YET

Chorus
An' I'll kiss thee yet, yet,
An' I'll kiss thee o'er again;
An' I'll kiss thee yet, yet,
My bonie Peggy Alison.

(Ilk Care and Fear, when thou art near,
I never mair defy them, O;
Young kings upon their hansel throne
Are no sae blest as I am, O!)

When in my arms wi' a' thy charms,
I clasp my countless treasures, O!
I seek nae mair o' Heav'n to share,
Than sic a moment's pleasure, O!

And by thy een sae bonie blue,
I swear I'm thine forever, O!
And on thy lips I seal my vow,
And break it I shall never, O!

ilk = every; hansel = good-luck; sic = such; een = eyes

Mally

We have absolutely no idea who Mally was. This may simply have been another old ballad rewritten by Burns, or it may have been a tribute to a passing fancy.

O MALLY'S MEEK, MALLY'S SWEET

Chorus
O Mally's meek, Mally's sweet,
Mally's modest and discreet,
Mally's rare, Mally's fair,
Mally's ev'ry way compleat.

As I was walking up the street,
A barefit maid I chanc'd to meet,
But O, the road was very hard
For that maiden's tender feet.

It were mair meet, that those fine feet
Were weel lac'd up in silken shoon,
And 'twere more fit that she should sit
Within yon chariot gilt aboon.

Her yellow hair, beyond compare,
Comes trinkling down her swan white neck,
And her two eyes like stars in skies
Would keep a sinking ship frae wreck.

shoon = shoes; aboon = above

Eliza Johnston

No one knows who this lady was. It is a very short epigram that suggests Eliza was merely a ship that passed in the night and was of little consequence to the Bard.

TO THE BEAUTIFUL MISS ELIZA JOHNSTON
ON HER PRINCIPLES OF LIBERTY AND EQUALITY

How Liberty, girl, can it be by thee nam'd?
Equality too! hussey, art not asham'd?
Free and Equal indeed; while mankind thou enchainest
And over their hearts a proud Despot so reignest.

Jean Jaffray

When Burns was travelling the country as an Exciseman he occasionally visited the manse in the village of Lochmaben. The minister's daughter was a young lady named Jean Jaffray to whom the following verses were dedicated. Jean eventually married and settled in New York, but she never forgot the wonderful evenings enjoyed by her family when Burns made his visits. She wrote later in her life:

I never could fancy that Burns had followed the rustic occupation of the plough, because everything he said or did had a gracefulness and charm that was in an extraordinary way engaging.

THE BLUE-EYED LASSIE

I gaed a waefu' gate, yestreen,
A gate, I fear, I'll dearly rue;
I gat my death frae twa sweet een,
Twa lovely een o' bonie blue.

'Twas not her golden ringlets bright,
Her lips like roses, wat wi' dew,
Her heaving bosom, lily-white,
It was her een sae bonie blue.

She talk'd, she smil'd, my heart she wyl'd,
She charm'd my soul I wist na how;
And ay the stound, the deadly wound,
Cam frae her een, sae bonie blue.

But spare to speak, and spare to speed;
She'll aiblins listen to my vow;
Should she refuse, I'll lay my dead
To her twa een sae bonie blue.

gaed = went; waefu' = woeful; gate = walk; een = eyes; aiblins = perhaps

Maggy

This appears to be an old ballad, probably rewritten by Burns, telling how the husband's feelings of love for his girlfriend soon change after marriage.

WHISTLE O'ER THE LAVE O'T

First when Maggy was in my care,
Heaven I thought was in her air;
Now we're married – spier nae mair,
Whistle o'er the lave o't.

Meg was meek, and Meg was mild,
Sweet and harmless as a child,
Wiser men than me beguil'd;
Whistle o'er the lave o't.

How we live, my Meg and me,
How we love and how we gree;
I care na by how few may see,
Whistle o'er the lave o't.

Wha I wish were maggot's meat,
Dish'd up in her winding-sheet;
I could write – but Meg maun see't.
Whistle o'er the lave o't.

spier nae mair = ask no more; lave = rest; winding-sheet = shroud

Mary

This is a soldier's farewell to his lover as he prepares to set off to a distant battlefield.

THE SILVER TASSIE

Go fetch to me a pint o' wine,
And fill it in a silver tassie;
That I may drink, before I go,
A service to my bonie lassie;
The boat rocks at the Pier o' Leith,
Fu' loud the wind blaws frae the Ferry,
The ship rides by the Berwick-law,
And I maun leave my bonie Mary.

The trumpets sound, the banners fly,
The glittering spears are ranked ready,
The shouts o' war are heard afar,
The battle closes deep and bloody.
It's not the roar o' sea or shore,
Wad make me langer wish to tarry;
Nor shouts o' war that's heard afar,
It's leaving thee, my bonie Mary!

tassie = goblet; the Ferry = Queensferry; maun = must; wad = would

Mrs Oswald

Not all the poems and songs written by Burns about women were kind and romantic. This particular piece was written in fury after he had been forced to give up his lodgings on a cold and stormy January night to make way for the funeral party of Mrs Oswald. Burns described the situation in a letter to Dr John Moore:

The inclosed ode is a compliment to the memory of the late Mrs Oswald of Auchencruive. You probably know her personally, an honor of which I cannot boast, but I spent my early years in her neighbourhood, and among her servants and tenants I know that she was detested with the most heart-felt cordiality. However, in the particular part of her conduct which aroused my Poetic wrath, she was much less blameable. In January last, on my road to Ayrshire, I had put up at Baillie Whigham's in Sanqhuar, the only tolerable inn in the place. The frost was keen, and the grim evening and howling wind were ushering in a night of snow and drift. My horse & I were both much fatigued with the labours of the day, and just as my friend the Baillie and I, were bidding defiance to the storm over a smoking bowl, in wheels the funeral pageantry of the late great Mrs Oswald, and poor I, am forced to brave all the horrors of the tempestuous night, and jade my horse, my young favorite horse whom I had just christened Pegasus, twelve miles farther on, through the wildest moors & hills of Ayrshire, to New Cumnock, the next Inn. The powers of Poesy & Prose sink under me, when I would describe what I felt. Suffice it to say, that when a good fire at New Cumnock had so far recovered my frozen sinews, I sat down and wrote the inclosed Ode ...

ODE, SACRED TO THE MEMORY OF MRS OSWALD OF AUCHENCRUIVE

Dweller in yon dungeon dark,
Hangman of creation, mark!
Who in widow weeds appears,
Laden with unhonoured years,
Noosing with care a bursting purse,
Baited with many a deadly curse?

STROPHE
View the wither'd beldam's face –
Can thy keen inspection trace
Aught of Humanity's sweet melting grace?
Note that eye,'tis rheum o'erflows,
Pity's flood there never rose.
See these hands, ne'er stretch'd to save,
Hands that took – but never gave.
Keeper of Mammon's iron chest,
Lo, there she goes, unpitied and unblest,
She goes, but not to realms of everlasting rest!

ANTISTROPHE

Plunderer of Armies, lift thine eyes,
(A while forbear, ye torturing fiends),
Sees thou whose step, unwilling, hither bends?
No fallen angel hurled from upper skies;
'Tis thy trusty quondam Mate,
Doomed to share thy fiery fate,
She, tardy, hell-ward plies.

EPODE

And are they of no more avail,
Ten thousand glittering pounds a year?
In other worlds can Mammon fail,
Omnipotent as he is here?
O, bitter mockery of the pompous bier,
While down the wretched vital part is driven!
The cave-lodged beggar, with a conscience clear,
Expires in rags, unknown, and goes to Heaven.

Mrs Frances Anna Dunlop

Mrs Frances Anna Dunlop appears to have been almost a mother figure to Burns. She was the widow of an aristocrat who was a direct descendant of William Wallace and had made herself known to the Bard by requesting six copies of the *Kilmarnock Edition* after she had read *The Cotter's Saturday Night*. Burns was highly flattered by this and wrote to Mrs Dunlop accordingly. This was to be the start of a long friendship and they corresponded on a regular basis. The letters were, however, far removed from the passionate epistles sent to Clarinda and more as he would have written to an elderly aunt. Burns also made several visits to the home of Mrs Dunlop over the years and was always a welcome guest within the household.

His first letter to Mrs Dunlop started thus:

Madam,

I am truly sorry I was not at home yesterday when I was so much honoured with your order for my Copies, and incomparably more so by the handsome compliments you are pleased to pay my poetic abilities. I am fully persuaded that there is not any class of Mankind so feelingly alive to the titillations of applause as the Sons of Parnassus; Nor is it easy to conceive how the heart of the poor Bard dances with rapture, when Judges honour him with their approbation. Had you been thoroughly acquainted with me, Madam, you could not have touched my darling heart-cord more sweetly, than by noticing my attempts to celebrate your illustrious Ancestor, the SAVIOUR OF HIS COUNTRY.

Although Burns appears to have kept his affair with Nancy McLehose a secret from Mrs Dunlop, he nevertheless sent her a copy of *Clarinda, Mistress of My Soul* for her approval. In a later letter he explains in great detail the history of his troubled relationship with Jean Armour, now reinstated as his wife:

Mrs Burns, Madam, is the identical woman who was the mother of twice twins to me in seventeen months. When she first found herself – 'As women wish to be who love their lords,' as I lov'd her near to distraction. I took some previous steps to a private marriage. – Her Parents got the hint; and in detestation of my guilt in being a poor devil, not only forbade me her company & their house, but on my rumoured West Indian voyage, got a warrant to incarcerate me in jail 'till I should find security in my about-to-be Paternal relation. – You know my lucky reverse of fortune. – On my eclatant return to Mauchline, I was made very welcome to visit my girl. – The usual consequences began to betray her; and as I was at that time laid up as a cripple in Edinburgh, she was turned, literally turned out of doors, and I wrote to a friend to shelter her, till my return. – I was not under the least verbal obligation to her, but her happiness or misery were in my hands, and who could trifle with such a deposite? …

And so the letters continued up to the year 1796 by which time something appears to have soured the relationship. However, the following lines were written to Mrs Dunlop on New Year's Day 1790 when they were still good friends:

SKETCH, NEW-YEAR'S DAY
TO MRS DUNLOP

This day, Time winds th' exhausted chain,
To run the twelvemonth's length again:
I see the old, bald-pated fellow,
With ardent eyes, complexion sallow,
Adjust the unimpair'd machine,
To wheel the equal, dull routine.

The absent lover, minor heir,
In vain assail him with their prayer,
Deaf as my friend, he sees them press,
Nor makes the hour one moment less.
Will you (the Major's with the hounds,
The happy tenants share his rounds;
Coila's fair Rachel's care today,
And blooming Keith's engaged with Gray;)
From housewife cares a minute borrow –
That grandchild's cap will do tomorrow –
And join with me a moralizing,
The day's propitious to be wise in.

First, what did yesternight deliver?
'Another year is gone forever.'
And what is this day's strong suggestion?
'The passing moment's all we rest on!'
Rest on – for what? What do we do here?
Or why regard the passing year?
Will time, amus'd with proverb'd lore,
Add to our date one minute more?
A few days may – a few years must –
Repose us in the silent dust.
Then is it wise to damp our bliss?
Yes – all such reasonings are amiss!
The voice of nature loudly cries,
And many a message from the skies,
That something in us never dies:
That on this frail, uncertain state,

Hang matters of eternal weight:
That future life in worlds unknown
Must take its hue from this alone;
Whether as heavenly glory bright,
Or dark as misery's woeful night –
Since then, my honor'd first of friends,
On this poor being all depends;
Let us the important now employ,
And live as those who never die.
Tho' you, with days and honors crown'd,
Witness that filial circle round,
(A sight life's sorrows to repulse,
A sight pale envy to convulse)
Others now claim your chief regard;
Yourself, you wait your bright reward.

Burns sent the following poem to Mrs Dunlop in 1790 as a note of condolence on the death of her son-in-law. However, he sent the same poem to Clarinda one year later claiming that he had only just composed it and changed the second line to begin 'Dearest Nancy':

ON SENSIBILITY

Sensibility, how charming,
Thou, my friend, cans't truly tell;
But distress with horrors arming,
Thou alas! has't known too well!

Fairest flower, behold the lily
Blooming in the sunny ray.
Let the blast sweep o'er the valley,
See it prostrate in the clay.

Hear the woodlark charm the forest,
Telling o'er his little joys:
Hapless bird! the prey the surest
To each pirate of the skies.

Dearly bought the hidden treasure,
Finer feelings can bestow;
Chords that vibrate sweetest pleasure,
Thrill the deepest notes of woe.

Mary

Although this beautiful song was written with reference to Mary, it is doubtful if any such person existed. It seems that the Bard was simply writing about his other love in life, Nature's beauty, and he certainly succeeded in producing a song that has spanned the years and remains eternally popular.

Burns wrote to Mrs Dunlop enclosing a copy of the song with the following note:

There is a small river, Afton, that falls into the Nith, near New Cumnock; which has some charming, wild, romantic scenery on its banks – I have a particular pleasure in those little pieces of poetry such as our Scotch songs &c. where the names of and landskip-features of rivers, lakes, or woodlands, that one knows are introduced. I attempted a compliment to the Afton as follows ...

AFTON WATER

Flow gently, sweet Afton, among thy green braes,
Flow gently, I'll sing thee a song in thy praise;
My Mary's asleep by thy murmuring stream,
Flow gently, sweet Afton, disturb not her dream.

Thou stock-dove whose echo resounds thro' the glen,
Ye wild whistling blackbirds in yon thorny den,
Thou green crested lapwing thy screaming forbear,
I charge you disturb not my slumbering Fair.

How lofty, sweet Afton, thy neighbouring hills,
Far mark'd with the courses of clear, winding rills;
There daily I wander as noon rises high,
My flocks and my Mary's sweet cot in my eye.

How pleasant thy banks and green vallies below,
Where wild in the woodlands the primroses blow;
There oft as mild ev'ning weeps over the lea,
The sweet scented birk shades my Mary and me.

Thy crystal stream, Afton, how lovely it glides,
And winds by the cot where my Mary resides;
How wanton thy waters her snowy feet lave,
As gathering sweet flowerets she stems thy clear wave.

Flow gently, sweet Afton, among thy green braes,
Flow gently, sweet River, the theme of my lays;
My Mary's asleep by thy murmuring stream,
Flow gently, sweet Afton, disturb not her dream.

birk = birch; cot = cottage

The Five Carlins

Although there are five women mentioned in this poem, they are all imaginary witches who give their opinions on candidates from the Whigs and the Tories competing for the position of parliamentary representative for the Dumfriesshire Burghs in September 1789. Burns was keenly interested in such affairs and had an amazing knowledge of each candidate. Once again he wrote to his friend, Mrs Dunlop, giving full details of each candidate but professing to be of no particular political persuasion:

> *I am too little a man to have any political attachments; I am deeply indebted to individuals of both parties; but a man who has it in his power to be the Father of a Country, and who is only known to that country by the mischiefs he does in it, is a character of which one cannot speak with patience ...*

Burns was obviously no fan of the Prince of Wales who had gained a position of great importance following his father's insanity.

There was five Carlins in the South,
They hit upon a scheme,
To send a lad to London town
To bring them tidings hame.

Not only bring them tidings hame,
But do their errands there;
And aiblins gowd and honor baith
Might be that laddie's share.

There was Maggie by the banks o' Nith,
A dame wi' pride enough;
And Marjory o' the many lochs,
A Carlin auld and teugh:

And blinkin Bess of Annandale,
That dwelt on Solway-side;
And Brandy Jean that took her gills
In Galloway sae wide:

And black Joan frae Crighton-peel,
O' gipsey kith and kin;
Five wighter Carlins were na found
The Sooth Coontrie within.

To send a lad to London town,
They met upon a day;
And mony a knight and mony a laird
That errand fain wad gae.

O mony a knight and mony a laird
That errand fain wad gae;
But nae ane could their fancy please,
O ne'er a ane but tway.

The first ane was a belted knight,
Bred of a Border band,
And he wad gae to London town,
Might nae man him withstand.

And he wad do their errands weel,
And meikle he wad say;
And ilka ane at London Court
Wad bid to him, Gude-day!

The niest came in a Sodger-boy
And spak wi' modest grace,
And he wad gang to London town
If sae their pleasure was.

He wad na hecht them courtly gifts,
Nor meikle speech pretend;
But he wad hecht an honest heart
Wad ne'er desert his friend.

Now wham to chuse, and wham refuse,
At strife thir Carlins fell;
For some had Gentle Folk to please,
And some wad please themsel.

Then up spak mim-mou'd Meg o' Nith,
And she spak up wi' pride,
And she wad send the Sodger-lad
Whatever might betide.

For the Auld Gudeman o' London Court,
　　She didna care a pin;
But she wad send the Sodger-lad
　　To greet his eldest son.

Then started Bess o' Annandale,
　　A deadly aith she's taen,
That she wad vote the Border-knight,
　　Tho' she should vote her lane.

'For far-off fowls hae feathers fair,
　　And fools o' change are fain;
But I hae try'd this Border-knight,
　　I'll try him yet again.'

Says black Joan frae Crighton-peel,
　　A Carlin stoor and grim;
'The Auld Gudeman, or the Young Gudeman,
　　For me may sink or swim.'

'For fools will prate o' Right and Wrang,
　　While knaves laugh them to scorn;
But the Sodger's friends hae blawn the best,
　　So he shall bear the horn.'

Then Brandy Jean spak o'er her drink,
　　'Ye weel ken, kimmers a',
The Auld Gudeman o' London Court,
　　His back's been at the wa';

'And mony a friend that kiss'd his caup,
　　Is now a fremit wight;'
But it's ne'er be sae wi' Brandy Jean,
　　'We'll send the Border knight.'

Then slow raise Marjory o' the lochs,
　　And wrinkled was her brow;
Her ancient weed was russet-grey
　　Her auld Scots heart was true.

'There's some Great Folk set light by me,
　　I set light by them;
But I will send to London town
　　Whom I lo'e best at hame.'

So how this weighty plea may end,
　　Nae mortal wight can tell;
God grant the king, and ilka man,
　　May look weel to themsel.

carlin = witch; aiblins = perhaps; gowd = gold; baith = both; teugh = tough; wighter = more powerful; fain = glad; meikle = much; niest = next; Sodger = soldier; hecht = promise; mim-mou'd = tight-mouthed; aith = oath; kimmers = gossips; caup = cup; fremit = aloof; wight = fellow

Margaret Burns

Margaret Burns was a celebrated Edinburgh prostitute whose activities in her Rose Street brothel had so offended the City Fathers that they had the unfortunate woman banished from Edinburgh to live the remainder of her life in a village outside the city boundary where she died three years later.

Although they shared the same surname, the Bard and Margaret Burns were not related, and Burns would never have demeaned himself by using the services of a lady of the streets. In fact, in his poem *The Fornicator* he pours scorn upon any man who would do this and declares that making love with a willing partner is what really counts.

However, the fate of Margaret Burns obviously angered the Bard as he wrote in a letter to a friend, Peter Hill:

How is the fate of my poor Namesake, Madamoiselle Burns, decided? Which of their grave Lordships can lay his hand upon his heart and say that he has not taken the advantage of such frailty; nay, if we may judge by near six-thousand years experience, can the World do without such frailty …

He continues:

As for these flinty-bosomed, puritannic Prosecutors of Female Frailty & Persecutors of Female Charms – I am quite sober – I am dispassionate … It is written 'Thou shalt not take the name of the Lord thy God in vain,' so I shall neither say God curse them! nor God blast them! nor God damn them! but may Woman curse them! may Woman blast them! may Woman damn them! May her lovely hand inexorably shut the Portal of Rapture to their most earnest Prayers & fondest essays for entrance.

TO THE MEMORY OF THE UNFORTUNATE MISS BURNS

Like to a fading flower in May,
Which Gardner cannot save,
So Beauty must, sometime, decay
And drop into the grave.

Fair Burns, for long the talk and toast
Of many a gaudy Beau,
That beauty has forever lost
That made each bosom glow.

Think fellow sisters on her fate!
Think, think how short her days!
Oh! think and e'er it be too late,
Turn from your evil ways.

Beneath this cold, green sod lies dead
That once bewitching dame
That fired Edina's lustful sons,
And quenched their glowing flame.

Written under the picture of the celebrated Miss Burns:

Cease, ye prudes, your envious railing,
Lovely Burns has charms – confess;
True it is she had one failing,
Had ae woman ever less?

Tibbie Dunbar

There is no reference to be found of anyone named Tibbie Dunbar, so we must assume that this was another ficticious female name used for rhyming purposes, or perhaps simply an old ballad revised by Burns.

O wilt thou go wi' me, sweet Tibbie Dunbar?
O wilt thou go wi' me, sweet Tibbie Dunbar?
Wilt thou ride on a horse, or be drawn in a car,
Or walk by my side, O sweet Tibbie Dunbar?

I care na thy daddie, his lands and his money;
I care na thy kin, sae high and sae lordly:
But say thou wilt hae me for better or waur,
And come in thy coatie, sweet Tibbie Dunbar.

Ann Masterton

Ann Masterton was the daughter of Allan Masterton, an Edinburgh school-teacher and writer of music, who had written several of the melodies for Burns' songs.

BEWARE O' BONIE ANN

Ye gallants bright I rede you right,
Beware o' bonie Ann;
Her comely face sae fu' o' grace,
Your heart she will trepan,
Her een sae bright, like stars by night,
Her skin is like the swan;
Sae jimply lac'd her genty waist,
That sweetly ye might span.

Youth, grace and love attendant move,
And pleasure leads the van;
In a' their charms and conquering arms,
They wait on bonie Ann.
The captive bands may chain the hands,
But love enslaves the man;
Ye gallants braw, I rede you a'
Beware o' bonie Ann.

rede = advise; trepan = ensnare; een = eyes; jimply = tightly; genty = neat

Eppie Adair

Yet another short song written about an unknown female. Probably an old ballad rewritten by the Bard.

Chorus
An' O, my Eppie,
My jewel, my Eppie!
Wha wad na be happy
Wi' Eppie Adair?

By Love, and by Beauty;
By Law, and by Duty;
I swear to be true to
My Eppie Adair!

A' pleasure exile me;
Dishonour defile me,
If e'er I beguile thee,
My Eppie Adair!

Mrs Sutherland

This lady was the wife of a gentleman who was in charge of a group of players who performed in the local theatre in Dumfries and who was about to open a new theatre in the town. Burns was very friendly with them and wrote this prologue for Mrs Sutherland to read at her Benefit Night in the theatre. Burns was a bit concerned about the political implications of this work and sent a copy to his friend, Provost Staig of Dumfries, to vet it for any passage that might be considered treasonable.

As he was involved at this time in his Excise duties, he had to be very wary about whose toes he might tread upon:

It is not for its merit that I trouble you with a copy of it ... but there is a dark stroke of Politics in the belly of the Piece, and like a faithful loyal Subject, I lay it before You, as the chief Magistrate of the Country, at least the only Magistrate whom I have met within the Country who had the honor to be very conspicuous as a Gentleman; that if the said Poem be found to contain any Treason, or words of treasonable construction, or any Fama clamosa or Scandalum magmatum, against our Sovereign lord the King, or any of his liege Subjects, the said Prologue may not see the light ...

SCOTS PROLOGUE FOR MRS SUTHERLAND'S BENEFIT NIGHT
SPOKEN AT THE THEATRE, DUMFRIES

What needs this din about the town o' Lon'on?
How this new Play and that new Sang is comin?
Why is outlandish stuff sae meikle courted?
Does Nonsense mend, like Brandy, when imported –
Is there nae Poet, burning keen for Fame,
Will bauldly try to gi'e us Plays at hame?
For Comedy abroad he need not toil,
A Knave and Fool are plants of ev'ry soil;
Nor need he hunt as far as Rome or Greece,
To gather matter for a serious piece;
There's themes enow in Caledonian story,
Wad shew the Tragic Muse in a' her glory.
Is there no darling Bard will rise and tell
How glorious Wallace stood, how hapless fell?
Where are the Muses fled that should produce
A drama worthy of the name of Bruce?
How on this spot he first unsheath'd the sword
'Gainst mighty England and her guilty Lord,
And after many a bloody, deathless doing,
Wrench'd his dear country from the jaws of Ruin!

O! for a Shakespeare or an Otway scene,
To paint the lovely, hapless Scottish Queen!
Vain ev'n the omnipotence of Female charms,
'Gainst headlong, ruthless, mad Rebellion's arms.
She fell – but fell with spirit truly Roman,
To glut that direst foe, – a vengeful woman;
A woman – tho' the phrase might seem uncivil,
As able – and as wicked as the devil!
(One Douglas lives in Home's immortal page,
But Douglases were heroes every age;
And tho' your fathers, prodigal of life,
A Douglas followed to the martial strife,
Perhaps, if bowls row right, and Right succeeds,
Ye yet may follow where a Douglas leads!)

As ye have generous done, if a' the land
Would take the Muses servants by the hand,
Not only hear, but patronise, defend them,
And where ye justly can commend – commend them;
And aiblins when they winna stand the test,
Wink hard, and say, 'The folks hae done their best.'
Would a' the land do this, then I'll be caition,
Ye'll soon hae Poets o' the Scottish nation,
Will gar Fame blaw until her trumpet crack;
And warsle Time, and lay him on his back.

For us and for our Stage should onie spier,
'Whase aught thae Chiels maks a' this bustle here?'
My best leg foremost, I'll set up my brow,
We have the honor to belong to you!
We're your ain bairns, e'en guide us as ye like,
But like guid mothers, shore before ye strike;
And grateful still, I trust ye'll ever find us:
For gen'rous patronage, and meikle kindness,
We've got frae a' professions, sorts and ranks;
God help us! – we're poor – ye'se get but thanks!

meikle = much; bauldly = boldly; aiblins = perhaps; caition = surety; gar = make; warsle = struggle;
spier = ask; whase aught thae chiels = whose are these people; ain bairns = own children; shore = warn

Mary Queen of Scots

Burns sent a copy of this poem to his friend Mrs Dunlop with the following note:

It is now near midnight, but I cannot resist the temptation my vanity, or, with respect to you, something perhaps more amiable than Vanity yet not quite so disinterested as Friendship, puts in my way to transcribe the following Ballad for you – it was finished only this day. – You know & with me, pity the amiable but unfortunate Mary Queen of Scots. To YOU and your YOUNG LADIES, I particularly dedicate the following Scots Stanzas –

He also sent a copy to his former sweetheart, Nancy McLehose:

Such, my dearest Nancy, were the words of the amiable but unfortunate Mary – Misfortune seems to take a peculiar pleasure in darting her arrows against 'Honest Men and bonie Lasses.' Of this, you are too, too such a proof, but may your future fate be a bright exception to the remark. – In the words of Hamlet – Adieu, adieu, adieu! Remember me!

LAMENT OF MARY QUEEN OF SCOTS ON THE APPROACH OF SPRING

> Now Nature hangs her mantle green
> On every blooming tree,
> And spreads her sheets o' daisies white
> Out o'er the grassy lea;
> Now Phoebus chears the crystal streams,
> And glads the azure skies;
> But nought can glad the weary wight
> That fast in durance lies.
>
> Now laverocks wake the merry morn,
> Aloft on dewy wing;
> The merle, in his noontide bower,
> Makes woodland echoes ring;
> The mavis mild wi' many a note,
> Sings drowsy day to rest;
> In love and freedom they rejoice,
> Wi' care nor thrall opprest.
>
> Now blooms the lily by the bank,
> The primrose down the brae;
> The hawthorn's budding in the glen,
> And milk-white is the slae;

The meanest hind in fair Scotland
May rove their sweets among;
But I, the Queen of a' Scotland,
Maun lie in prison strang.

I was the Queen o' bonie France,
Where happy I hae been;
Fu' lightly rase I on the morn,
As blithely lay down at e'en;
And I'm the sovereign of Scotland,
And mony a traitor there;
Yet here I lie in foreign bands,
And never ending care.

But as for thee, thou false woman,
My sister and my fae,
Grim vengeance yet, shall whet a sword
That thro' thy soul shall gae;
The weeping blood in woman's breast
Was never known to thee;
Nor th' balm that draps on wounds o' woe
Frae woman's pitying e'e.

My son! my son! may kinder stars
Upon thy fortune shine!
And may those pleasures gild thy reign,
That ne'er wad blink on mine!
God keep thee frae thy mother's faes,
Or turn their hearts to thee:
And where thou meet'st thy mother's friend,
Remember him for me!

O! soon to me, may summer-suns
Nae mair light up the morn!
Nae mair, to me, the autumn winds
Wave o'er the yellow corn!
And in the narrow house o' death
Let winter round me rave;
And the next flowers that deck the spring,
Bloom on my peaceful grave.

laverocks = larks; merle = hawk; maun = must; rase = rose; false woman = Queen Elizabeth I; fae = foe; wad = would

Anna Park

Anna Park was the niece of the landlady of the Globe Inn, Dumfries where she was employed as a barmaid. Robert Burns was a regular visitor to the Globe and soon became entranced with Anna. It is believed that Anna had a reputation for offering her customers more than what she was serving from the bar, but that did not prevent the Bard from his pursuit of her, which, incidentally, is the only recorded affair he had since renewing his marriage to Jean Armour.

Burns may not have been a successful farmer, but when it came to sewing his own wild oats, he seems to have been remarkably fecund and Anna became pregnant. The affair ended with Anna giving birth to a daughter which Burns presented to his wife, Jean, a mere nine days before she herself gave birth to another child. It is uncertain what became of Anna. She had fled to Leith to have the child but we do not know if she died in childbirth or survived and stayed to live in that part of the country. Jean accepted the child into her family as one of her own declaring that 'Rab should hae twa wives'.

Burns considered the following song to be one of his finest works.

THE GOWDEN LOCKS OF ANNA

Yestreen I had a pint o' wine,
A place where body saw na;
Yestreen lay on this breast o' mine
The gowden locks of Anna.
The hungry Jew in wilderness
Rejoicing o'er his manna,
Was naething to my hiney bliss
Upon the lips of Anna.

Ye Monarchs take the East and West,
Frae Indus to Savannah!
Gi'e me within my straining grasp
The melting form of Anna.
There I'll despise Imperial charms,
An Empress or Sultana.
While dying raptures in her arms
I give and take with Anna!!!

Awa, thou flaunting god o' day!
Awa, thou pale Diana!
Ilk star, gae hide thy twinkling ray!
When I'm to meet my Anna.

Come, in thy raven plumage, Night;
Sun, moon and stars withdrawn a';
And bring an angel pen to write
My transports wi' my Anna.

Postscript

The kirk and state may join and tell;
To do sic things I maunna;
The kirk and state may go to hell,
And I shall gae to Anna.
She is the sunshine o' my e'e,
To live but her I canna;
Had I on earth but wishes three,
The first should be my Anna.

Yestreen = last night; gowden = golden; ilk = each; sic = such; maunna = must not; canna = cannot

Eliza Burnet

Eliza Burnet was the daughter of Lord Monboddo and became acquainted with Robert Burns during his period in Edinburgh. She sadly died from consumption at the age of 24. Burns was very impressed by Eliza and mentioned her in his *Address to Edinburgh*, and it seems that their closeness was commented upon by the gossiping ladies in Edinburgh society. Their menfolk were similarly disposed to assume that Eliza and Robert were up to no good.

One apparently stated that she had very bad teeth while another commented on the thickness of her ankles. However, we know by now that Burns was blind to any imperfection in a woman he admired.

He sent a copy of the Address to William Chalmers with the following comments:

Fair B – is the heavenly Miss Burnet, daughter to Lord Monboddo, at whose house I have had the honor to be more than once. There has not been anything nearly like her, in all the combinations of Beauty, Grace and Goodness the great Creator has formed since Milton's Eve on the first day of her existence …

Some months after her death Burns wrote to Mrs Dunlop:

I do not remember if I ever mentioned to you my having an idea of composing an Elegy on the late Miss Burnet of Monboddo. I had the honor of being pretty well acquainted with her, & have seldom felt so much at the loss of an acquaintance as when I heard that so amiable & accomplished a piece of God's works was no more …

A FRAGMENT
MEANT FOR THE BEGINNING OF AN ELEGY ON
THE LATE MISS BURNET OF MONBODDO

Life ne'er exulted in so rich a prize,
As Burnet lovely from her native skies;
Nor envious Death so triumph'd in a blow,
As that which laid th' accomplish'd Burnet low.

Thy form and mind, sweet Maid! can I forget,
In richest ore the brightest jewel set!
In thee, what Heaven above, was truest shown,
For by his noblest work the Godhead best is known.

In vain ye flaunt in summer's pride, ye groves;
Thou crystal streamlet with thy flowery shore,
Ye woodland choir that chant your idle loves,
Ye cease to charm, Eliza is no more.

Ye heathy wastes immix'd with reedy fens,
Ye mossy streams with sedge and rushes stor'd,
Ye rugged cliffs o'erhanging dreary glens,
To you I fly, ye with my soul accord.

Princes whose cumbrous pride was all their worth,
Shall venal lays their pompous exit hail;
And thou, sweet Excellence! forsake our earth,
And not a Muse in honest grief bewail!

We saw thee shine in youth and beauty's pride,
And virtue's light that beams beyond the spheres;
But like the sun eclips'd at morning tide
Thou left'st us darkling in a world of tears.

The Parent's heart that nestled fond in thee,
That heart how sunk a prey to grief and care!
So deckt the woodbine sweet yon aged tree;
So, rudely ravish'd, left it bleak and bare.

Deborah Duff Davies

This young lady was a friend of the Riddells, Burns' good friends in Mauchline. She was yet another young lady who was greatly admired by the Bard and was another lost to consumption while still in the bloom of her life. She was the subject of several works by the Bard, and was also the recipient of several letters from him. The letters, however, were very formal, as Burns apparently was aware of the social distance that lay between them. Here are one or two extracts:

Why, dear Madam, must I wake up from this delightful reverie & find it is all a dream? Why, amid my generous enthusiasm, must I find myself a poor, powerless devil, incapable of wiping a tear from the eye of Misery, or adding one comfort to the Friend I love ...

And in the same letter:

Still, the inequalities of life are, among MEN, comparatively tolerable, but there is a DELICACY, a TENDERNESS, accompanying every view in which one can place lovely WOMAN, that are grated and shocked at the rude, capricious distinction of Fortune. WOMAN is the BLOOD-ROYAL of life: let there be slight degrees of precedency among them, but let them all be sacred.

LOVELY DAVIES

O how shall I, unskilfu', try
The Poet's occupation?
The tunefu' Powers, in happy hours,
That whisper, inspiration,
Even they maun dare an effort mair
Than aught they ever gave us,
Or they rehearse in equal verse
The charms o' lovely Davies.

Each eye it chears when she appears,
Like Phoebus in the morning,
When past the shower, and every flower
The garden is adorning;
As the wretch looks o'er Siberia's shore,
When winter-bound the wave is;
Sae droops our heart when we maun part
Frae charming, lovely Davies.

Her smile's a gift frae boon the lift,
That maks us mair than princes;
A scepter'd hand, a king's command,
Is in her darting glances:
The man in arms 'gainst female charms,
Even he her willing slave is;
He hugs his chain, and owns the reign
Of conquering lovely Davies.

My Muse to dream of such a theme,
Her feeble powers surrender;
The eagle's gaze alane surveys
The sun's meridian splendour:
I wad in vain essay the strain,
The deed too daring brave is;
I'll drap the lyre, and mute, admire
The charms o' lovely Davies.

maun = must; frae = from; boon the lift = beyond the horizon; alane = alone; drap = drop

Burns continued his adulation of the diminutive Deborah with the following song which has remained a favourite at Burns Suppers ever since.

BONIE WEE THING

Chorus
Bonie wee thing, cannie wee thing,
Lovely wee thing, was thou mine;
I wad wear thee in my bosom,
Least my Jewel I should tine.

Wishfully I look and languish
In that bonie face o' thine;
And my heart it stounds wi' anguish,
Least my wee thing na be mine.

Wit, and Grace, and Love, and Beauty,
In ae constellation shine,
To adore thee is my duty,
Goddess o' this soul o' mine!.

EPIGRAM ON MISS DAVIES

Ask why God made the GEM so small,
And why so huge the granite?
Because God meant, mankind should set
The highest value on it.

Lesley Baillie

Lesley Baillie was a near neighbour of Burns' friend and confidante, Mrs Dunlop. In a lengthy epistle sent to Mrs Dunlop in August 1792, Burns waxes lyrical about Lesley:

> *... do you know that I am almost in love with an Acquaintance of yours. 'Almost!' said I – I am in love, souse! Over head and ears, deep as the most unfathomable abyss of the boundless ocean; but the word 'Love,' owing to the intermingledoms of the good and bad, the pure and impure, in this world, being rather an equivocal term for expressing ones sentiments and sensations, I must do justice to the sacred purity of my attachment. Know, then, that the heart-struck awe, the distant humble approach; the delight we should have in gazing upon and listening to a Messenger from Heaven, appearing in all the unspotted purity of his Celestial Home, among the coarse, polluted, far inferior sons of men, to deliver them tidings that made their hearts swim in joy and their imaginations soar in transport – such, so delighting, and so pure, were the emotions of my soul on meeting the other day with Miss Lesley Baillie, your neighbour at Mayfield ...*

O SAW YE BONIE LESLEY

O saw ye bonie Lesley,
As she gaed o'er the border?
She's gane like Alexander,
To spread her conquests farther.

To see her is to love her,
And love but her forever;
For Nature made her what she is
And never made anither.

Thou art a queen, fair Lesley,
Thy subjects we, before thee;
Thou art divine fair Lesley,
The hearts o' men adore thee.

The deil he could na scaith thee,
Or aught that wad belang thee;
He'd look into thy bonie face,
And say, 'I canna wrong thee!'

The Powers aboon will tent thee,
Misfortune sha' na steer thee;
Thou'rt like themsels sae lovely,
That ill they'll ne'er let near thee.

Return again, fair Lesley,
Return to Caledonie!
That we brag, we hae a lass
There's nane again sae bonie.

gaed = went; gane = gone; could na scaith = could not harm; aboon = above; tent = tend; steer = afflict

Burns' admiration for Lesley continued, and with a second song he wrote to his publisher, George Thomson:

'Blythe hae I been o'er the hill' *which is one of the finest Songs ever I made in my life; & besides is composed on a young lady, positively the most beautiful, lovely woman in the world.*

And in a letter enclosing a copy of the song to Lesley:

Among your sighing swains, if there should be one whose ardent sentiment & ingenuous modesty fetter his powers of speech in your presence; with that look and attitude so native to your manner, & of all others the most bewitching – Beauty listening to Compassion – put my Ballad in the poor fellow's hand, just to give a little breathing to the fervour of his soul …

BLYTHE HAE I BEEN ON YON HILL

Blythe hae I been on yon hill,
As the lambs beside me;
Careless ilka thought and free,
As the breeze flew o'er me;
Now nae longer sport and play,
Mirth or sang can please me;
Lesley is sae fair and coy,
Care and anguish seize me.

Heavy, heavy is the task,
Hopeless love declaring;
Trembling, I dow nocht but glowr,
Sighing, dumb, despairing!
If she winna ease the thraws,
In my bosom swelling;
Underneath the grass-green sod
Soon maun be my dwelling.

ilka = each; dow nocht but glowr = dare only stare; winna = will not; thraws = frustrations; maun = must

Jenny

Robert Burns detested the practice of arranged marriages in which dowries were paid by suitors to the parents of young girls. He believed firmly that the only base for marriage was love.

WHAT CAN A YOUNG LASSIE DO WI' AN AULD MAN

What can a young lassie, what shall a young lassie,
What can a young lassie do wi' an auld man?
Bad luck on the pennie, that tempted my Minnie
To sell her poor Jenny for siller and lan'!

He's always compleenin frae morning to e'enin,
He hoasts and he hirpls the weary day lang:
He's doyl't and he's dozin, his blude it is frozen,
O, dreary's the night wi' a crazy auld man!

He hums and he hankers, he frets and he cankers,
I never can please him, do a' that I can;
He's peevish, and jealous of a' the young fellows,
O, dool on the day I met wi' an auld man!

My auld auntie Katie upon me taks pity,
I'll do my endeavour to follow her plan;
I'll cross him, and wrack him until I heartbreak him,
And then his auld brass will buy me a new pan.

Minnie = mother; siller = money; hoasts = coughs; hirpls = limps; doyl't = senile; hums = mumbles; hankers = loiters; cankers = complains; dool = woe

Eppie McNab

Eppie McNab is a character from an old bawdy ballad, rewritten and cleaned up by Burns.

O saw ye my dearie, my Eppie McNab?
O saw ye my dearie, my Eppie McNab?
She's down in the yard, she's kissin the Laird,
She winna come hame to her ain Jock Rab.

O come thy ways to me, my Eppie McNab;
O come thy ways to me, my Eppie McNab;
What-e'er thou has done, be it late be it soon,
Thou's welcome again to thy ain Jock Rab.

What says she, my dearie, my Eppie McNab?
What says she, my dearie, my Eppie McNab?
She lets thee to wit, that she has thee forgot,
And for ever disowns thee, her ain Jock Rab.

O had I ne'er seen thee, my Eppie McNab!
O had I ne'er seen thee, my Eppie McNab!
As light as the air, and fause as thou's fair,
Thou's broken the heart o' thy ane Jock Rab!

winna = will not; ain = own; fause = false

Bessy and Her Spinning-wheel

In sharp contrast to his poems dedicated to young women, this beautiful piece is written in tribute to the beauties of nature and the simplicity of a bygone age. Here he describes the scene surrounding Bessy the countrywoman as she sits quietly at her spinning-wheel in order to provide all the clothing that she requires. It is a beautifully composed picture in words that also derides the activities of the rich and great.

O leeze me on my spinnin-wheel,
And leeze me on my rock and reel;
Frae tap to tae that cleeds me bien,
And haps me fiel and warm at e'en!
I'll set me down and sing and spin,
While laigh descends the simmer sun,
Blest wi' content, and milk and meal,
O leeze me on my spinnin-wheel.

On ilka hand the burnies trot,
And meet below my theekit cot;
The scented birk and hawthorn white
Across the pool their arms unite,
Alike to screen the birdie's nest,
And little fishes' callor rest:
The sun blinks kindly in the biel',
Where, blythe I turn my spinnin-wheel.

On lofty aiks the cushats wail,
And Echo cons the doolfu' tale;
The lintwhites in the hazel braes,
Delighted, rival ithers lays:
The craik amang the claver hay,
The pairtrick whirrin o'er the ley,
The swallow jinkin round my shiel,
Amuse me at my spinnin-wheel,

Wi' sma' to sell, and less to buy,
Aboon distress, below envy,
O wha wad leave this humble state,
For a' the pride of a' the Great?

Amid their flairing, idle toys,
Amid their cumbrous, dinsome joys,
Can they the peace and pleasure feel
Of Bessy at her spinnin-wheel!

leeze = bless; frae tap to tae = from top to bottom; cleeds = clothes; haps = covers ; fiel = warm; laigh = low; ilka = each; burnies = streams; theekit cot = thatched cottage; birk = birch; callor = cool; biel' = shelter; aiks = oaks; cushats = wood-pigeons; doolfu' = doleful; lintwhites = linnets; craik = corncrake; claver = clover; pairtrick = partridge; ley = meadow; jinkin = darting; shiel = shed; aboon = above; wad = would

Mistress Jean

Robert Burns was a great collector of old Scots ballads, many of which were bawdy in the extreme. This one relates to life in a mining village in Ayrshire and tells how the young lass refuses to be tempted away from her true love by the promise of riches and servants.

MY COLLIER LADDIE

Whare live ye, my bonie lass,
And tell me how they ca' ye?
My name she says, is Mistress Jean,
And I follow my Collier laddie,

See you not yon hills and dales
The sun shines on sae brawlie?
They are a' mine and they shall be thine,
Gin ye'll leave your Collier laddie.

Ye shall gang in gay attire,
Weel buskit up sae gaudy;
And ane to wait on every hand,
Gin ye'll leave your Collier laddie.

Tho' ye had a' the sun shines on,
And the earth conceals sae lowly;
I wad turn my back on you and it a',
And embrace my Collier laddie.

I can win my five pennies in a day
And spen't at night fu' brawlie;
And make my bed in the Collier's neuk,
And lie down wi' my Collier laddie.

Love for love is the bargain for me,
Tho' the wee Cot-house should haud me;
And the warl' before me to win my bread,
And fair fa' my Collier laddie!

weel buskit up sae gaudy = well dressed; gin = if; neuk = corner; Cot-house = cottage; haud = hold

121

The Shepherd's Wife

Another example of an old, bawdy ballad being breathed upon by the Bard. This time the wife is using her feminine guile to tempt her husband to return home.

The Shepherd's wife cries o'er the knowe,
Will ye come hame, will ye come hame;
The Shepherd's wife cries o'er the knowe,
Will ye come hame again een, jo?

What will I get to my supper,
Gin I come hame, gin I come hame?
What will I get to my supper,
Gin I come hame again een, jo?

Ye'se get a panfu' o' plumpin parridge,
And butter in them, and butter in them,
Ye'se get a panfu' o' plumpin parridge,
Gin ye'll come hame again een, jo.

Ha, ha, how! that's naething that dow.
I winna come hame, I canna come hame;
Ha, ha, how! that's naething that dow,
I winna come hame gin een, jo.

A reekin fat hen, weel fryth'd i' the pan,
Gin ye'll come hame, gin ye'll come hame,
A reekin fat hen weel fryth'd i' the pan,
Gin ye'll come hame again een, jo.

A weel made bed and a pair o' clean sheets,
Gin ye'll come hame, gin ye'll come hame,
A weel made bed and a pair o' clean sheets,
Gin ye'll come hame again een, jo.

A luvin wife in lily-white linens,
Gin ye'll come hame, gin ye'll come hame,
A luvin wife in lily-white linens,
Gin ye'll come hame again een, jo.

Ha, ha, how! that's something that dow,
  I will come hame, I will come hame;
Ha, ha, dow! that's something that dow,
  I will come hame again een, jo.

knowe = knoll; jo = darling; gin = if; dow = can; reekin = steaming

Fair Eliza

Although this piece is addressed to Fair Eliza, it seems that it was originally written for someone by the name of Rabina, but was altered before going to press. It also appears that Burns invited Johnson to tell him of any female whom he may wish to have celebrated in verse, and he, Burns, would oblige.

In a letter to Johnson dated August 1788, he wrote:

Have you never a fair goddess that leads you a wild-goose chase of amorous devotion? Let me know a few of her qualities, such as she be rather, black or fair, plump or thin, short or tall, &c. & chuse your air, & I shall task my Muse to celebrate her.

Turn again, thou fair Eliza,
Ae kind blink before we part;
Rew on thy despairing Lover,
Canst thou break his faithfu' heart!
Turn again, thou fair Eliza,
If to love thy heart denies,
For pity hide the cruel sentence
Under friendship's kind disguise!

Thee, sweet maid, hae I offended?
The offence is loving thee:
Canst thou wreck his peace for ever,
Wha for thine wad gladly die!
While the life beats in my bosom,
Thou shalt mix in ilka throe;
Turn again thou lovely maiden,
Ae sweet smile on me bestow.

Not the bee upon the blossom,
In the pride o' sinny noon;
Not the little sporting fairy,
All beneath the simmer moon;
Not the Poet in the moment
Fancy lightens in his e'e.
Kens the pleasure, feels the rapture,
That thy presence gi'es to me.

Ae kind blink = a loving glance; sinny = sunny; kens = knows

May

In a letter to George Thomson, Burns made the comment:

The Posie is my composition; the air was taken down from Mrs Burns's voice. It is well known in the West Country, but the old words are trash ...

THE POSIE

O luve will venture in where it daur na weel be seen,
O luve will venture in where wisdom ance has been;
But I will down yon river rove, amang the woods sae green,
And a' to pu' a posie to my ain dear May.

The primrose I will pu', the firstling o' the year;
And I will pu' the pink, the emblem o' my Dear,
For she is the pink o' womankind, and blooms without a peer;
And a' to be a posie to my ain dear May.

I'll pu' the budding rose when Phoebus peeps in view,
For it's like a baumy kiss o' her sweet, bonie mou;
The hyacinth's for constancy, wi' its unchanging blue,
And a' to be a posie to my ain dear May.

The lily it is pure, and the lily it is fair,
And in her lovely bosom I'll place the lily there;
The daisy's for simplicity and unaffected air,
And a' to be a posie to my ain dear May.

The hawthorn I will pu' wi' its locks o' siller grey,
Where like an aged man it stands at break o' day;
But the songster's nest within the bush I winna tak away;
And a' to be a posie to my ain dear May.

The woodbine I will pu' when the e'ening star is near,
And the diamond draps o' dew shall be her een sae clear;
The violet's for modesty which weel she fa's to wear,
And a' to be a posie to my ain dear May.

I'll tie the posie round wi' the silken band o' luve,
And I'll place it in her breast, and I'll swear by a' abuve,
That to my latest draught o' life the band shall ne'er remuve,
And this will be the posie to my ain dear May.

daur na = dare not; ain = own; baumy = balmy; mou = mouth; winna = will not

Willie's Wife

This is very different to the poems and songs written about the many beautiful young women Burns loved to celebrate. It is written in the old style of grotesquerie, which was very popular in Scotland.

SIC A WIFE AS WILLIE HAD

Willie Wassle dwalts on Tweed,
  The spot they ca' it Linkumdoddie;
A creeshie wabster till his trade,
  Can steal a clue wi' ony body:
He has a wife that's dour and din,
  Tinkler Madgie was her mither;
    Sic a wife as Willie's wife,
    I wadna gi'e a button for her.

She has an e'e, she has but ane,
  Our cat has twa, the very colour;
Five rusty teeth, forbye a stump,
  A clapper-tongue wad deave a miller:
Her whiskin beard about her mou,
  Her nose and chin they threaten ither;
    Sic a wife as Willie's wife,
    I wadna gi'e a button for her.

She's bow-hough'd, she's hem-shin'd,
  Ae limpin leg a hand-breed shorter;
She's twisted right, she's twisted left,
  To balance fair in ilka quarter:
She has a hump upon her breast,
  The twin o' that upon her shouther;
    Sic a wife as Willie's wife,
    I wadna gi'e a button for her.

Auld baudrans by the ingle sits,
  And wi' her loof her face is washin;
But Willie's wife is nae sae trig,
  She dights her grunzie wi' a hushion:

Her walie knieves like midden-creels,
Her feet wad fyle the Logan-water;
Sic a wife as Willie's wife,
I wadna gi'e a button for her.

wabster = weaver; din = stubborn; sic = such; deave = deafen; mou = mouth; bow-hough'd = bandy-legged; hem-shin'd = shins like a horse-collar; hand-breed = hand's breadth; ilka = each; shouther = shoulder; auld baudrans = old cat; loof = paw; nae sae trig = not so trim; dights her grunzie = wipes her mouth; hushion = footless stocking; walie knieves = large fists; midden-creels= muck buckets; fyle = foul

Lady Mary Ann

This is possibly an old folk song picked up by Burns on his Highland tour and amended by him. It certainly does not feel like the work of the Bard.

MY BONIE LADDIE'S YOUNG BUT HE'S GROWIN YET

O Lady Mary Ann looked o'er the castle-wa',
She saw three bonie boys playin at the ba'
The youngest he was the flower amang them a',
My bonie laddie's young but he's growin yet.

O Father, O Father, an' ye think it fit,
We'll send him a year to the College yet,
We'll sew a green ribbon round his hat,
And that will let them ken he's to marry yet.

Lady Mary Ann was a flower in the dew,
Sweet was its smell and bonie was its hue,
And the langer it blossom'd, the sweeter it grew,
For the lily in the bud will be bonier yet.

Young Charlie Cochran was the sprout of an aik,
Bonie, and bloomin and straught was its make,
The sun took delight to shine for its sake,
And it will be the brag o' the forest yet.

The Simmer is gane when the leaves they were green,
And the days are awa that we hae seen;
But far better days I trust will come again,
For my bonie laddie's young but he's growin yet.

ken = know; aik = oak; straught = straight; gane = gone

Bonie Bell

This piece falls into the same category as the previous one. Again there is an air of uncertainty as to whether this was actually written by Burns. We have no idea of the identity of Bonie Bell.

The smiling spring comes in rejoicing,
And surly winter grimly flies;
Now crystal clear are the falling waters,
And bonie blue are the sunny skies.
Fresh o'er the mountains breaks forth the morning,
The ev'ning gilds the Ocean's swell;
All Creatures joy in the sun's returning,
And I rejoice in my Bonie Bell.

The flowery Spring leads sunny Summer,
And yellow Autumn presses near,
Then in his turn comes gloomy Winter,
Till smiling Spring again appear.
Thus seasons dancing, life advancing,
Old Time and Nature their changes tell,
But never ranging, still unchanging,
I adore my Bonie Bell.

Miss Fontenelle

Louisa Fontenelle was a London actress whose performances on stage with Sutherland's Company delighted Burns. He wrote the *Rights of Woman* as an address for her to use on her Benefit Night, which he enclosed with the following letter that also included a flattering, short poem on the lady herself:

Madam,

In such a bad world as ours, those who add to the scanty sum of our pleasures, are positively our Benefactors. To you, Madam, on our humble Dumfries boards, I have been more indebted for entertainment, than ever I was in prouder Theatres. Your charms as a woman would insure applause to the most indifferent Actress, & your theatrical talents would secure admiration to the plainest figure. This Madam, is not the unmeaning, or insidious compliment of the Frivolous or Interested. I pay it from the same honest impulse that the Sublime of Nature excites my admiration, or her beauties give me delight.

Will the foregoing words be of any service to you on your approaching benefit night? If they will, I shall be prouder of my Muse than ever. They are nearly extempore; I know they have no great merit; but though they shall add but little to entertainment of the evening, they give me the happiness of an opportunity to declare how much I have the honor to be.

Madam, your very humble servant.

ON SEEING MISS FONTENELLE IN A FAVOURITE CHARACTER

Sweet naivete of feature,
Simple, wild, enchanting elf,
Not to thee, but thanks to nature,
Thou art acting but thyself.

Wert thou awkward, stiff, affected,
Spurning nature, torturing art;
Loves and graces all rejected,
Then indeed thou'd act a part.

THE RIGHTS OF WOMAN

While Europe's eye is fixed on mighty things,
The fate of Empires and the fall of Kings;
While quacks of State must each produce his plan,
And even children lisp The Rights of Man;
Amid this mighty fuss, just let me mention,
The Rights of Woman merit some attention.
First, in the sexes' intermixed connection,
One sacred Right of Woman is, Protection.
The tender flower that lifts its head elate,
Helpless, must fall before the blasts of Fate,
Sunk on the earth, defac'd its lovely form.
Unless your Shelter ward th' impending storm.

Our second Right – but needless here is caution,
To keep that Right inviolate's the fashion.
Each man of sense has it so full before him,
He'd die before he'd wrong it – 'tis Decorum.
There was, indeed, in far less polished days,
A time when rough, rude man had naughty ways;
Would swagger, swear, get drunk, kick up a riot,
Nay, even thus invade a lady's quiet.
Now, thank our Stars! these Gothic times are fled,
Now well-bred men (and you are all well-bred)
Most justly think (and we are all the gainers)
Such conduct neither spirit, wit nor manners.

For Right the third, our last, our best, our dearest,
That Right to fluttering Female hearts the nearest,
Which even the Rights of Kings, in low prostration,
Most humbly own – 'tis dear, dear Admiration!
(In that blest sphere alone we live and move;
There taste that life of life – immortal love.)
Smiles, glances, sighs, tears, fits, flirtations, airs;
'Gainst such an host, what flinty savage dares,
When aweful Beauty joins in all her charms,
Who is so rash as rise in rebel arms?

But truce with kings, and truce with Constitutions,
With bloody armaments and Revolutions;
Let Majesty your first attention summon,
Ah, ca ira! The Majesty of Woman!!!

It is worth noting that Burns wrote the above address more than 150 years before women in Great Britain were allowed to vote, and during a period in history when women were regarded as mere chattels.

A year later he sent her another address with another flowery letter to accompany it:

Inclosed is the 'Address,' such as it is; & may it be a prologue to an overflowing House! If all the Town put together, have half the ardour for your success & welfare, of my individual wishes, my prayer will most certainly be granted. Were I man of gallantry & fashion, strutting & fluttering in the foreground of the picture of Life, making the speech to a lovely young girl might be construed to be one of the doings of All-powerful-Love; but you will be surprised, my dear Madam, when I tell you that it is not Love, nor even Friendship, but sheer Avarice. In all my jostlings & jumblings, windings & turnings, in life, disgusted at every corner, as man with the least taste & sense must be, with vice, folly, arrogance, imper-tinence, nonsense & stupidity, my soul has ever, involuntarily & instinctively, selected as it were for herself, a few whose regard, whose esteem, with a Miser's Avarice she wished to appropriate & preserve. It is truly from this cause, ma chere Madamoiselle, that any, the least, service I can be of to you, gives me most real pleasure. God knows I am a powerless individual. And when I thought on my Friends, many a heart-ache it has given me! But if Miss Fontenelle will accept this honest compliment to her personal charms, amiable manner & gentle heart, from a man, too proud to flatter, though too poor to have his compliments of any consequence, it will sincerely oblige her anxious Friend, & most devoted and humble servant.

Jean Lorimer

Jean Lorimer was the daughter of a farmer who lived about two miles from Ellisland. She was obviously a very attractive young lady as her father's farm became a popular calling place for Burns and his fellow Excisemen. Burns started off by writing a song about her on behalf of one of his colleagues who had hoped to marry Jean, but this proved to be in vain as she fled to Gretna Green to marry a local wastrel instead. This was a disastrous move on her part, as her new husband fled three weeks after the wedding, leaving Jean to face his creditors. Jean returned home to the farm, but her misfortunes followed as her father became bankrupt forcing them to move to Dumfries.

She became a regular visitor to the Burns' house in the town and was the inspiration for many poems and songs written by the Bard, who referred to her as 'Chloris' in several pieces. Burns was obviously attracted to Jean Lorimer, but there is no proof of any relationship having developed between them. The words of passion contained in so many of the large number of poems and songs which he wrote in her honour, however, would suggest that their relationship was deeper than that of mere friendship.

Burns sent the first song to George Thomson with the plea:

If it suits you to insert it, I shall be pleased, as the heroine is a favorite of mine ...

POORTITH CAULD

O poortith cauld, and restless love,
Ye wrack my peace between ye;
Yet poortith a' I could forgive
An' 'twere na for my Jeanie.

Chorus
O why should Fate sic pleasure have,
Life's dearest bands untwining;
Or why sae sweet a flower as love,
Depend on Fortune's shining?

This warld's wealth when I think on,
Its pride, and a' the lave o't;
My curse on silly coward man,
That he should be the slave o't!

Her een sae bonie blue betray,
How she repays my passion;
But Prudence is her o'erword ay,
She talks o' rank and fashion.

O wha can prudence think upon,
And sic a lassie by him?
O wha can prudence think upon,
And sae in love as I am?

How blest the wild-wood Indian's fate,
He woos his simple Dearie;
The silly bogles, Wealth and State,
Can never make them eerie.

poortith = poverty; cauld = cold; lave = rest; o'erward = byword; ay = ever; bogles = evil spirits; eerie = scared

This next song, which also features Jean Lorimer as the central character, has remained one of the Bard's most popular pieces over the years.

WHISTLE AN' I'LL COME TO YE, MY LAD

Chorus
O whistle, and I'll come to ye, my lad,
O whistle, and I'll come to ye, my lad;
Tho' father, and mother, and a' should gae mad,
Thy Jeanie will venture wi' ye, my lad.

But warily tent, when ye come to court me,
An' come nae unless the back-yet be a-jee;
Syne up the back-style and let naebody see
And come as ye were na comin to me,
And come as ye were na comin to me.

At kirk, or at market when'er ye meet me,
Gang by me as tho' that ye car'd nae a flie;
But steal me a blink o' your bonie black e'e.
Yet look as ye were na looking at me,
Yet look as ye were na looking at me.

Ae vow and protest that ye care na for me,
And whyles ye may lightly my beauty a wee;
But court nae anither, tho' jokin ye be,
For fear that she wyle your fancy frae me,
For fear that she wyle your fancy frae me.

warily tent = be careful; yet = gate; a-jee = ajar; may lightly my beauty a wee = talk about me in a flattering manner

COME LET ME TAKE THEE

Come, let me take you to my breast,
And pledge we ne'er shall sunder;
And I shall spurn, as vilest dust,
The warld's wealth and grandeur:
And do I hear my Jeanie own,
That equal transports move her?
I ask for dearest life alone
That I may live to love her.

Thus in my arms, wi' a' thy charms,
I clasp my countless treasure;
I seek nae mair o' Heaven to share,
Than sic a moment's pleasure;
And by thy een, sae bonie blue,
I swear I'm thine forever!
And on thy lips I seal my vow,
And break it shall I never!

Burns' infatuation with Jean Lorimer continued as he wrote a letter to Alexander
Cunningham explaining to him about Chloris:

*Written on the blank leaf of a copy of the last edition of my Poems, presented to the lady
whom in so many fictitious reveries of Passion but with the most ardent sentiments of real
friendship, I have so often sung under the name of – CHLORIS.*

THINE AM I, MY CHLORIS FAIR

Thine am I, my Chloris fair,
Well thou may'st discover;
Every pulse along my veins
Tells the ardent Lover.

To thy bosom lay my heart,
There to throb and languish:
Tho' Despair had wrung its core,
That would heal the anguish.

Take away these rosy lips,
Rich with balmy treasure:
Turn away thine eyes of love,
Lest I die with pleasure!

What is Life when wanting Love?
Night without a morning:
Love's the cloudless summer sun,
Nature gay adorning.

TO CHLORIS

Ah, Chloris, since it may not be,
That thou of love wilt hear;
If from the lover thou maun flee,
Yet let the friend be dear.

Altho' I love my Chloris, mair
Than ever tongue could tell;
My passion I will ne'er declare,
I'll say, I wish thee well.

Tho' a' my daily care thou art,
And a' my nightly dream,
I'll hide the struggle in my heart,
And say it with esteem.

maun = must

ON CHLORIS
REQUESTING ME TO GIVE HER A SPRAY OF
A SLOE-THORN IN FULL BLOSSOM

From the white blossom'd sloe, my dear Chloris requested
A sprig, her fair breast to adorn;
No, by Heavens! I replied, let me perish forever,
Ere I plant in that bosom a thorn!

ON HEARING CHLORIS BEING ILL

Chorus
Long, long the night,
Heavy comes the morrow,
While my soul's delight
Is on her bed of sorrow.

Can I cease to care?
Can I cease to languish?
While my darling Fair
Is on the couch of anguish?

Ev'ry hope is fled;
Ev'ry fear is terror;
Slumber even I dread,
Ev'ry dream is horror.

Hear me. Powers Divine!
Oh, in pity, hear me!
Take aught else of mine,
But my Chloris spare me.

'TWAS NA HER BONIE BLUE E'E

'Twas na her bonie blue e'e was my ruin;
Fair tho' she be, that was ne'er my undoing;
'Twas the dear smile when naebody did mind us,
'Twas the bewitching, sweet, stown glance o' kindness.

Sair do I fear that to hope is denied me,
Sair do I fear that despair maun abide me;
But tho' fell Fortune should fate us to sever,
Queen shall she be in my bosom forever.

Chloris I'm thine wi' a passion sincerest,
And thou hast plighted me love o' the dearest!
And thou'rt the angel that never can alter,
Sooner the sun in his motion would falter.

stown = stolen; sair = sore; maun abide me = must live with me

MARK YONDER POMP

Mark yonder pomp of costly fashion,
Round the wealthy, titled bride;
But when compar'd with real passion,
Poor is all that princely pride.
What are their showy treasures?

What are their noisy pleasures?
The gay, gaudy glare of vanity and art;
The polish'd jewel's blaze
May draw the wond'ring gaze,
And courtly grandeur bright
The fancy may delight,
But never, never can come near the heart.

But did you see my sweetest Chloris,
In simplicity's array;
Lovely as yonder sweet opening flower is,
Shrinking from the gaze of day.
O then, the heart alarming,
And all resistless charming,
In Love's delightful fetters, she chains the willing soul!

Ambition would disown
The world's imperial crown,
Even Av'rice would deny
His Worship's deity,
And feel thro' every vein love's raptures roll.

FORLORN MY LOVE, NO COMFORT HERE

Chorus
O wert thou, Love but near me,
But near, near, near me
How kindly thou woulds't chear me,
And mingle sighs with mine, Love.

Forlorn my Love, no comfort near,
Far, far from thee I wander here;
Far, far from thee the fate severe
At which I most repine, Love.

Around me scowls a wintry sky,
Blasting each bud of hope and joy;
And shelter, shade, nor home have I ,
Save in these arms of thine, Love.

Cold, alter'd friends with cruel art
Poisoning fell Misfortune's dart;
Let me not break thy faithful heart,
And say that fate is mine, Love.

But dreary tho' the moments fleet,
O let me think we yet shall meet!
That only ray of solace sweet
Can on thy Chloris shine, Love!

Burns' infatuation with Jean Lorimer seemed endless, but at last we reach the final poem to Chloris.

O, BONIE WAS YON ROSY BRIER

O, bonie was yon rosy brier,
That blooms sae far frae haunt o' man;
And bonie she, and ah, how dear!
It shaded frae the e'enin sun.

Yon rosebuds in the morning dew
How pure, amang the leaves sae green;
But purer was the lover's vow
They witness'd in their shade yestreen.

All in its rude and prickly bower
That crimson rose how sweet and fair;
But love is far a sweeter flower
Amid life's thorny path o' care.

The pathless wild, and wimpling burn,
Wi' Chloris in my arms, be mine;
And I thee warld nor wish nor scorn,
Its joys and griefs alike resign.

Jessie Staig

Jessie Staig was the daughter of the Provost of Dumfries and would seem to have suffered ill-health for most of her short life. Her grave lies a few short steps from Burns' mausoleum in St Michael's Kirkyard, Dumfries. Burns felt sympathy towards her and her family as he wrote to Mrs Dunlop:

Ah, my dear Madam, the feelings of a Parent are not to be described! I sympathised much, the other day, with a father, a man whom I respect highly. He is Mr Staig, the leading man in our Borough. A girl of his, a lovely creature of sixteen, was given over by the Physician, who openly said that she had but few hours to live. A gentleman who also lives in the town, and who had studied medicine in the first schools, the Dr Maxwell whom Burke mentioned in the House of Commons about the affair of the daggers – he was at last called in; & his prescriptions, in a few hours altered her situation and have now cured her. Maxwell is my most intimate friend & one of the first characters I have ever met with ...

Dr Maxwell was later to suggest the cure for Burns' condition was to stand immersed in the freezing waters of the Brow Well on the coast of the Solway Firth up to his neck ... a remedy that hastened his death.

YOUNG JESSIE

True hearted was he, the sad swain o' the Yarrow,
And fair are the maids on the banks o' the Ayr;
But by the sweet side o' the Nith's winding river,
Are lovers as faithful, and maidens as fair:
To equal young Jessie, seek Scotland all over;
To equal young Jessie, you seek it in vain:
Grace, Beauty and Elegance fetter her lover,
And maidenly modesty fixes the chain.

Fresh is the rose, in the gay, dewy morning,
And sweet is the lily at evening close;
But in the fair presence o' lovely, young Jessie,
Unseen is the lily, unheeded the rose.
Love sits in her smile, a wizard ensnaring;
Enthron'd in her een he delivers his law;
And still to her charms she alone is a stranger,
Her modest demeanour's the jewel of a'.

Burns wrote the following lines to Dr Maxwell about Jessie:

TO DR MAXWELL, ON MISS JESSIE STAIG'S RECOVERY

Maxwell, if merit here you crave,
That merit I deny:
You saved fair Jessie from the grave!
An Angel could not die.

Maria Riddell

Maria Riddell was a member of a wealthy family with whom Burns enjoyed an excellent relationship. She was a very literate young lady who had written a book based on her travels to the West Indies where she had met her husband. The Bard's friendship with Maria came to a sudden and dramatic end, however, when he was attending a party at the home of her sister-in-law, Elizabeth Riddell, in December 1793. Many versions of what occurred on that fateful evening have been ventured, so it is difficult to know the precise facts. Apparently, some of the men in attendance decided it would be fun to re-enact *The Rape of the Sabine Women*, and Burns is reputed to have overacted his part with the hostess, Elizabeth Riddell, resulting in him being ordered to leave the house in disgrace.

Another theory is that Burns may have been set up by some of the young army officers in attendance, in revenge for him describing them as 'lobster-coated puppies', but we'll never know. Burns was deeply ashamed over this turn of events and wrote a lengthy letter to Elizabeth, to express his remorse. It begins:

Madam,

I dare say this is the first epistle you ever received from the nether world. I write you from the regions of Hell, amid the horrors of the damned. The time and manner of my leaving your earth I do not exactly know, as I took my departure in the heat of a fever of intoxication, contracted at your too hospitable mansion: but on my arrival here, I was fairly tried and sentenced to endure the purgatorial tortures of this infernal confine for the space of ninety-nine years, eleven months, and twenty-nine days, and all on account of the impropriety of my conduct yesternight under your roof. Here am I laid on a bed of pitiless furze, with my aching head laid on a pillow of everpiercing thorn, while an infernal tormentor, wrinkled and old, and cruel, his name, I think is Recollection, with whip of scorpions, forbids peace or rest to approach me, and keeps anguish eternally awake …

Now, it may seem odd that the following poem is written to Eliza when the subject is Maria, but there is an explanation. Burns had written it to compliment Maria Riddell, but after the fracas sent a revised copy to Mrs Dunlop, having altered the name from Maria to Eliza.

FAREWELL, THOU STREAM

Farewell, thou stream that winding flows
Around Eliza's dwelling;
O mem'ry, spare the cruel throes
Within my bosom swelling;
Condemn'd to drag a hopeless chain,
And yet in secret languish;
To feel a fire in every vein,

Nor dare disclose my anguish.
Love's veriest wretch, unseen, unknown
I fain my grief would cover;
The bursting sigh, th' unweeting groan,
Betray the hapless lover:
I know thou doom'st me to despair,
Nor wilt, nor canst relieve me;
But, Oh Eliza, hear one prayer,
For pity's sake forgive me!

The music of thy voice I heard,
Nor wist while it enslav'd me;
I saw thine eyes, yet nothing fear'd,
'Till fears no more had saved me;
Th' unwary sailor, thus aghast,
The wheeling torrent viewing,
Mid circling horrors sink at last
In overwhelming ruin.

This short epigram is undated, so it is unclear if it was written before or after the fall-out.

TO MARIA

'Praise Woman still!' his Lordship says,
'Deserved, or not, no matter,'
But thee Maria, while I praise,
There Flattery cannot flatter.

Maria, all my thoughts and dream,
Inspire my vocal shell;
The more I praise my lovely Theme
The more the truth I tell.

Burns was not a man who enjoyed being crossed and was capable of attacking in verse anyone who he considered had offended him. Maria Riddell now came into that category and he wrote to his beloved Clarinda about her:

The subject of the foregoing is a woman of fashion in this country, with whom, at one period, I was well acquainted. By some scandalous conduct to me, & two or three other gentlemen here as well as me, she steered so far to north of my good opinions, that I have made her the theme of several ill-natured things. The following Epigram struck me the other day, as I passed her carriage …

EPIGRAM PINNED TO MRS RIDDELL'S CARRIAGE

If you rattle along like your Mistresses tongue,
　　Your speed will outrival the dart:
But, a fly for your load, you'll break down on the road,
　　If your stuff be as rotten's her heart.

MONODY ON MARIA

How cold is that bosom which folly once fired,
How pale is that cheek where the rouge lately glistened;
How silent that tongue which the echoes oft tired,
How dull is that ear which to flattery listened.

If sorrow and anguish their exit await,
From friendship and dearest affection removed;
How doubly severer, Maria, thy fate,
Thou diedst unwept, as thou livedst unloved.

Loves, Graces, and Virtues, I call not on you;
So shy, grave and distant, ye shed not a tear;
But come all ye offspring of folly so true,
And flowers let us cull for Maria's cold bier.

We'll search through the garden for each silly flower,
We'll range through the forest for each idle weed;
But chiefly the nettle, so typical, shower,
For none e'er approached her but rued the rash deed.

We'll sculpture the marble, we'll measure the lay;
Here Vanity strums on her idiot lyre;
Here keen Indignation shall dart on his prey,
Which spurning Contempt shall redeem from his ire.

THE EPITAPH

Here lies, now a prey to insulting Neglect
What once was a butterfly gay in life's beam:
Want only of wisdom denied her respect,
Want only of goodness denied her esteem.

And still the attack continued. Esopus was an Ancient Roman actor who Burns used to depict James Williamson, the manager of a travelling theatre company that played occasionally at Dumfries. When the troupe was playing at Whitehaven, the Earl of Lonsdale imprisoned all the members of the troupe as vagrants. Williamson had also been part of the Riddell social circle and Burns used this poem to attack both Maria Riddell and the Earl of Lonsdale. It is a difficult poem to follow as it contains many oblique references to historical figures.

FRAGMENT – EPISTLE FROM ESOPUS TO MARIA

From these drear solitudes and frowzy Cells,
Where Infamy with sad repentance dwells;
Where Turnkeys make the jealous portal fast,
Then deal from iron hands the spare repast;
Where truant 'prentices, yet young in sin,
Blush at the curious stranger peeping in;
Where strumpets, relics of the drunken roar,
Resolve to drink – nay half, to whore – no more;
Where tiny thieves, not destined yet to swing,
Beat hemp for others riper for the string:
From these dire scenes my wretched lines I date,
To tell Maria her Esopus fate.
'Alas, I feel I am no actor here!'
'Tis real Hangmen real scourges bear.
Prepare Maria, for a horrid tale
Will turn thy very rouge to deadly pale;
Will make thy hair, tho' erst from gipsey poll'd,
By Barber woven and by Barber sold,
Tho' twisted smooth by Harry's nicest care,
Like Boary bristles to erect and stare.
The hero of the mimic scene, no more
I start in Hamlet, in Othello roar;
Or haughty Chieftain, mid the din of arms,
In highland bonnet woo Malvina's charms;
While Sans Culotes stoop up the mountain high
And steal from me Maria's prying eye.
Blest highland bonnet, once my proudest dress!
Now, prouder still, Maria's temples press!
I see her wave thy tow'ring plumes afar,
And call each Coxcomb to the wordy war.
I see her face the first of Ireland's sons,
And even out-Irish his Hibernian bronze.

The Crafty Colonel, leaves the tartan'd lines
For other wars, where He a hero shines;
The hopeful youth in Scottish Senate bred,
Who owns a Bushby heart without the head,
Comes mid a string of coxcombs, to display
The veni, vidi, vici is his way.
The shrinking Bard adown an alley skulks,
And dreads a meeting worse than Woolwich hulks
Tho' there his heresies in Church and State
Might well award him Muir and Palmer's fate;
Still she, undaunted, reels and rattles on,
And dares the public like a noonday sun!

What scandal call'd Maria's jaunty stagger
The ricket reeling of a crooked swagger?
What slander nam'd her seeming want of art
The flimsey wrapper of a rotten heart
Whose spite e'en worse than Burns's venom when
He dips in gall unmixed his eager pen,
And pours his vengeance in the burning line?
Who christen'd thus Maria's Lyre divine,
The idiot strum of vanity bemused,
And e'en th' abuse of poesy abused?
Who called her verse a parish workhouse, made
For motely, foundling fancies, stolen or strayed?

A Workhouse! ah, that thorn awakes my woes,
And pillows on the thorn my racked repose!
In durance vile here must I wake and weep,
And all my frowzy Couch in sorrow steep;
That straw where many a rogue has lain of yore,
And vermin'd Gipseys litter'd heretofore.
Why Lonsdale, thus thy wrath on Vagrants pour?
Must Earth no Rascal save thyself endure?
Must thou alone in crimes immortal swell,
And make a vast Monopoly of Hell?
Thou knowest the Virtues cannot hate thee worse;
The Vices also, must they club their curse?
Or must no tiny sin to others fall,
Because thy guilt's supreme enough for all?
Maria, send me too thy griefs and cares;
In all of thee, sure, thy Esopus shares.

As thou at all mankind the flag unfurls,
Who on my fair one Satire's vengeance hurls?
Who calls thee pert, affected, vain Coquette,
A wit in folly and a fool in wit?
Who says that Fool alone is not thy due,
And quotes thy treacheries to prove it true?
Our force united on thy foes we'll turn,
And dare the war with all of woman born;
For who can write and speak as thou and I
My periods that deciphering defy,
And thy still matchless tongue that conquers all reply.

The war between Burns and the Riddells eventually ended when Maria sent him a book for his perusal a year later. It must be remembered that Maria was only 21 at the time and was probably missing the companionship of Burns. They had been sufficiently friendly for him to be seen in her box at the theatre on several occasions, but family loyalty would have played a large part in her cutting Burns from her social circle.

In his return letter to Maria he writes:

Tis true, Madam, I saw you once since I was at Woodley park; & that once froze the very life-blood of my heart. Your reception of me was such, that a wretch, meeting the eye of his Judge, about to pronounce sentence of death upon him, could only have envied my feelings and situation. But I hate the theme; & never more shall write or speak of it.

Happily the friendship began to flourish once more as can be seen in another letter written in March 1794:

I cannot help laughing at your friend's conceit of my picture; & I suspect you are playing off on me some of that fashionable wit, called HUMBUG. Apropos to pictures, I am just sitting to Reid in the town for a miniature; & I think he has hit by far the best likeness of me ever was taken. When you are at any time so idle, in town, as to call at Reid's painting-room, & mention to him that I spoke of such a thing to you, he will shew it to you; else he will not; For both the miniature's existence & its destiny, are an inviolable secret, & therefore very properly trusted in part to you.

Maria Riddell proved to be a good friend to Robert Burns and his family, for after his death she set about ensuring the welfare of Jean Armour and the children.

Her own life suffered badly as her husband failed to pay for the estate in which she lived causing her to move to a much lesser dwelling. She eventually remarried but died in 1808 at the age of 36.

Meg o' the Mill

Robert Burns was adamant in his belief that no amount of wealth or worldly goods could ever compensate for love in a marriage, as he states so clearly in this piece.

KEN YE WHAT MEG O' THE MILL HAS GOTTEN

O ken ye what Meg o' the mill has gotten,
An' ken ye what Meg o' the mill has gotten?
She's gotten a coof wi' a claut o' siller,
And broken the heart o' the barley Miller.

The Miller was strappin', the Miller was ruddy,
A heart like a lord, and a hue like a lady;
The Laird was a widdefu', bleerit knurl;
She's left the gude-fellow and taen the churl.

The Miller he hecht her, a heart leal and luving,
The Laird did address her wi' matter mair muving
A fine pacing horse wi' a clear chained bridle,
A whip by her side, and a bonie side-saddle.

O wae on the siller. It is so prevailing,
And wae on the luve that's fix'd on a mailin!
A tocher's nae word in a true luver's parle,
But gi'e me my luve, and a fig for the warl!

ken = know; coof = dolt; claut o' siller = horde of money; widdefu' bleerit knurl = gallows-worthy
bleary-eyed dwarf; churl = miserable person; hecht = offered; leal = loyal; mair = more; wae = woe;
siller = silver; mailin = farm; tocher = dowry; parle = speech; warl = world

Jean McMurdo

Jean McMurdo was the daughter of a friend of the Bard, and he wrote the following poem in her honour, although there is a suspicion that it may have really been intended for his wife, Jean Armour. Ever the one to offer advice on life to young people about to enter the adult world, Burns wrote this rather long-winded letter to Jean, as she reached her 16th birthday, in which he compares her to the daughter in *The Cotter's Saturday Night*. It is interesting to note how the Bard was alarmed at the actions of the young women in that era, proving once again that nothing in life really changes.

Madam,

Amid the profusion of complimentary address which your age, sex, & accomplishments will now bring you, permit me to approach you with my devoirs, which, however deficient may be their consequence in other respects, have the double novelty & merit, in these frivolous, hollow times of being poetic & sincere. In the inclosed ballad I have, I think, hit off a few outlines of your portrait. The personal charms, the purity of mind, the ingenuous naivete of heart & manners, in my heroine, are, I flatter myself, a pretty just likeness of Miss McMurdo in a Cottage. Every composition of this kind must have a series of dramatic incident in it; so I have had recourse to my invention to finish the rest of the ballad.

So much for the Poet: now let me add a few wishes which every man who has the honor of himself being a father, must breathe, when he sees female Youth, Beauty & Innocence about to enter into this much chequered world & very precarious world. May you, my young Madam, escape that FRIVOLITY which threatens universally to pervade the minds & manners of Fashionable life. To pass by the rougher, & still more degenerate Sex; the mob of Fashionable Female Youth, what are they? Are they any thing? They prattle, laugh, sing, dance, finger a lesson, or perhaps turn over the leaves of a fashionable Novel, but are their minds stored with any information, worthy of the noble powers of reason & judgement; or do their hearts glow with Sentiment, ardent, generous & humane? Were I to poetise on the subject, I would call them the butterflies of the human kind, remarkable only for & distinguished only by, the idle variety of their gaudy glare, silly straying from one blossoming weed to another, without a meaning & without an aim; the idiot prey of every pirate of the skies, who thinks them worth his while as he wings his way by them; & speedily, by wintry Time, swept to that oblivion whence they might as well never have appeared.

Amid this crowd of Nothing, may you, Madam, be Something! May you be a Character, dignified as Rational & Immortal being.

A still more formidable plague in life, unfeeling interested Selfishness; is a contagion too impure to touch you. The selfish drift to bless yourself alone; to build your fame on another's ruin; to look on the child of Misfortune without commiseration, or even the victim of Folly without pity – these, & every other feature of a heart rotten at the core, are what you are totally incapable of. These wishes, Madam, are of no consequence to you, but to me they are of the utmost; as they give me an opportunity of declaring with what respect I have the honor to be.

&c.

149

BONIE JEAN

There was a lass and she was fair,
At kirk and market to be seen;
When a' our fairest maids were met,
The fairest maid was bonie Jean.

And ay she wrought her Mammie's wark,
And ay she sang sae merrily;
The blythest bird upon the bush
Had ne'er a lighter heart than she.

But hawks will rob the tender joys
That bless the little lintwhite's nest;
And frost will blight the fairest flowers,
And love will break the soundest rest.

Young Robie was the brawest lad,
The flower and pride of a' the glen;
And he had owsen, sheep and kye,
And wanton naigies nine or ten.

He gaed wi' Jeanie to the tryste,
He danc'd wi' Jeanie on the down;
And lang e'er witless Jeanie wist,
Her heart was tint, her peace was stown.

As in the bosom o' the stream
The moon-beam dwells at dewy e'en;
So, trembling, pure was tender love,
Within the breast o' bonie Jean.

And now she works her Mammie's wark,
And ay she sighs wi' care and pain;
Yet wist not what her ail might be,
Or what wad mak her weel again.

But did na Jeanie's heart lowp light,
And did na joy blink in her e'e;
As Robie told a tale o' love,
Ae e'enin on the lily lea.

The sun was sinking in the west,
The birds sweet in ilka grove;
His cheek to hers he fondly laid,
And whisper'd thus his tale o' love.

O Jeanie fair, I lo'e thee dear,
O canst thou think to fancy me!
Or wilt thou leave thy Mammie's cot,
And learn to tent the farms wi' me.

At barn or byre thou shalt not drudge,
Or naething else to trouble thee;
But stray amang the heather-bells,
And tent the waving corn wi' me.

Now what could artless Jeanie do?
She had nae will to say him na;
At length she blush'd a sweet consent,
And love was ay between them twa.

wark = work; lintwhite's = linnet; brawest = finest; owsen = oxen; kye = cattle; naigies = horses; gaed = went; tryste = market; wist = knew; tint = lost; stown = stolen; ail = ailment; wad = would; lowp = leap; cot = cottage

Phillis

This unremarkable piece was written about Phillis McMurdo, one of the 14 McMurdo children.

PHILLIS THE FAIR

While larks with little wing, fann'd the pure air,
Viewing the breathing spring, forth did I fare:
Gay the sun's golden eye peep'd o'er the mountains high;
Such thy morn! did I cry, Phillis the fair.

In each bird's careless song, glad I did share;
While yon wild flowers among, chance led me there:
Sweet to the opening day, rosebuds bent the dewy spray;
Such thy bloom, did I say, Phillis the fair.

Down in a shady walk, doves cooing were;
I marked the cruel hawk caught in a snare:
So kind may Fortune be, such make his destiny!
He would injure thee, Phillis the fair.

Burns wrote another song about Phillis to please a friend of his who wished to impress the girl.

ADOWN WINDING NITH

Chorus
Awa wi' your Belles and your Beauties,
They never wi' her can compare;
Wha-ever has met wi' my Phillis
Has met wi' the Queen o' the Fair

Adown winding Nith I did wander,
To mark the sweet flowers as they spring;
Adown winding Nith I did wander,
Of Phillis to muse and to sing.

The Daisy amus'd my fond fancy,
So artless, so simple, so wild;
Thou emblem, said I, o' my Phillis,
For she is simplicity's child

The rose-bud's the blush o' my Charmer,
   Her sweet balmy lips when 'tis prest;
How fair and how pure is the lily,
   But fairer and purer her breast.

Yon knot of gay flowers in the arbour,
   They ne'er wi' my Phillis can vie;
Her breath is the breath o' the woodbine,
   Its dew-drop o' diamond, her eye.

Her voice is the songs of the morning,
   That wake thro' the green-spreading grove,
When Phoebus peeps over the mountains
   On music, and pleasure, and love.

But Beauty, how frail and how fleeting,
   The bloom of a fine summer's day;
While Worth in the mind of my Phillis
   Will flourish without a decay.

Annie

Burns was sitting under a tree studying some old ballads when he decided that the words of *Allan Water* were unworthy of such a lovely tune. He rewrote the words to his own satisfaction, stating that 'it was not done in my worst style'.

Annie appears to be no more than a name that probably came with the old ballad and has no significance at all.

ALLAN WATER

By Allan-side I chanced to rove,
While Phoebus sank beyond Benledi;
The winds were whispering thro' the grove,
The yellow corn was waving ready;
I listen'd to a lover's sang,
And thought on youthfu' pleasures mony;
And ay the wild-wood echoes rang
O dearly do I lo'e thee, Annie.

O happy is the woodbine bower,
Nae nightly bogle make it eerie;
Nor ever sorrow stain the hour,
The place and time I met my Dearie!
Her head upon my throbbing breast,
She, sinking said, 'I'm thine forever!'
While mony a kiss the seal imprest,
The sacred vow, we ne'er should sever.

The haunt o' Spring's the primrose-brae,
The Simmer joys the flocks to follow;
How cheery, thro' her shortening day,
Is Autumn in her weeds o' yellow;
But can they melt the glowing heart,
Or chain the soul in speechless pleasure,
Or thro' each nerve the rapture dart,
Like meeting Her, our bosom's treasure.

bogle = ghost

Mary

George Thomson wrote a letter of admonishment to Burns asking him to amend a stanza in one of his poems. Thomson wrote:

I wish you would invoke the muse for a single elegant stanza to be substituted for the concluding objectionable verses of Down the Burn, Davie, *so that this most exquisite song no longer be excluded from good company.*

The verse which offended him so greatly was as follows:

As down the burn they took their way,
What tender tales they said!
His cheek to hers he aft did lay
And with her bosom play'd.

Burns was not happy with this alteration but eventually succumbed to the will of Thomson and rewrote the verse.

DOWN THE BURN, DAVIE

As down the burn they took their way,
And thro' the flowery dale;
His cheek to hers he aft did lay,
And love was ay the tale.

With 'Mary, when shall we return,
Sic pleasure to renew;'
Quoth Mary, 'Love, I like the burn,
And ay shall follow you.'

Jenny

Burns sent this song to Janet Miller of Dalswinton, daughter of his former landlord, with the following letter:

Madam, I have taken the liberty to make you the Heroine of the Song on the foregoing page. Being little in the secret of young ladies' loves & lovers – how should I, you know? I have formed in my fancy a little love-story for you; & a lamentable ditty I have put in your Lover's mouth. The air, you know, is excellent, & the verses. I hope, & think, are in my best manner. It goes into Pleyel's songs; & allows me to tell you a truth (what your Sex, Youth & Charms from my Sex, may not often hear) I am sincerely happy to having an opportunity of shewing, with what respect I have the honor to be,

> *Madam,*
> *Your very humble servant*
> *Robt Burns*

FAIR JENNY

Where are the joys I have met in the morning,
    That danced to the lark's early song?
Where is the peace that awaited my wand'ring,
    At evening the wild-woods among?

No more a winding the course of yon river,
    And marking sweet flowerets so fair;
No more I trace the light footsteps of Pleasure,
    But Sorrow and sad-sighing Care.

Is it that Summer's forsaken our vallies,
    And grim, surly Winter is near?
No, no! the bees humming round the gay roses
    Proclaim it the pride of the year.

Fain would I hide, what I fear to discover,
    Yet long, long too well have I known;
All that has caused this wreck in my bosom,
    Is Jenny, fair Jenny alone.

Time cannot aid me, my griefs are immortal,
    Not Hope dare a comfort bestow;
Come then, enamour'd and fond of my anguish,
    Enjoyment I'll seek in my woe.

Anne Graham

Yet another simple poem written to please a friend, this time the subject was the daughter of a patron, Robert Graham of Fintry.

TO MISS GRAHAM OF FINTRY

Here, where the Scottish Muse immortal lives,
In sacred strains and tuneful numbers join'd.
Accept the gift; though humble he who gives,
Rich is the tribute of the grateful mind.

So may no ruffian feeling in the breast
Discordant jar thy bosom-chords among;
But Peace attune thy gentle soul to rest,
Or love ecstatic wake his seraph song.

Or Pity's notes, in luxury of tears,
As modest want the tale of woe reveals;
While conscious Virtue all her strain endears,
And heaven-born Piety her sanction seals.

Lady Elizabeth Heron

Burns was seldom impressed by the many songs and poems which he received from members of the aristocracy, but he made an exception with Lady Elizabeth Heron of Heron, daughter of the Earl of Dundonald, and in a letter to Thomson, wrote:

> *I know you value a Composition, because it is made by one of the Great Ones, as little as I do. However, I got an air, pretty enough composed by Lady Elizabeth Heron of Heron, which she calls the* Banks of Cree. *Cree is a beautiful, romantic stream, & as her Ladyship is a particular friend of mine, I have written the following song to it.*

THE BANKS OF CREE

Here is the glen, and here is the bower,
All underneath the birchen shade;
The village-bell has told the hour,
O what can stay my lovely maid.

'Tis not Maria's whispering call;
'Tis but the balmy breathing gale,
Mixt with some warbler's dying fall
The dewy star of eve to hail.

It is Maria's voice I hear;
She calls the woodlark in the grove
His little, faithful Mate to chear,
At once 'tis music – and 'tis love.

And thou art come! and thou art true!
O welcome dear to love and me!
And let us all our vows renew
Along the flowery banks of Cree.

Chloe

George Thomson was constantly telling Burns to concentrate more on English songs, presumably to widen the range of his market, but Burns was loath to change his style. Indeed, his ventures into English tend to be weak affairs compared to his natural usage of the Scots dialect.

He wrote to Thomson in November 1794 with the following comments:

Despairing of my own powers to give you variety enough in English Songs, I have been turning over old Collections to pick out songs of which the measure is something similar to what I want, & with a little alteration so as to suit the rhythm of the air exactly, to give you them for your Work. Where the Songs have hitherto been little noticed, nor have been set to music, I think the shift a fair one.

SONG ALTERED FROM AN OLD ENGLISH ONE

It was the charming month of May,
When all the flowers were fresh and gay,
One morning, by the break of day,
The youthful, charming Chloe;
From peaceful slumber she arose,
Girt on her mantle and her hose,
And o'er the flowery mead she goes,
The youthful, charming Chloe.

Chorus
Lovely was she by the dawn,
Youthful Chloe, charming Chloe,
Tripping o'er the pearly lawn,
The youthful, charming Chloe.

The feather'd people, you might see,
Perch'd all round on every tree,
In notes of sweetest melody,
They hail the charming Chloe;
Till, painting gay the eastern skies,
The glorious sun began to rise,
Out rivall'd by the radiant eyes
Of youthful, charming Chloe.

Philly

How could a song written for George Thomson and his wife, Katherine, become entitled *Philly and Willy*? The answer lies in a letter written by Burns to George Thomson in 1794 as he expounds upon a song that he has written:

I once set about verses for it, which I meant to be in the alternative way of a lover & his Mistress chanting together. I have not the pleasure of knowing Mrs Thomson's christian name, & yours I am afraid to say is rather burlesque for sentiment, else I had meant to have made you the hero & heroine of the little piece …

Burns decided that the name Katherine was unpoetic, but Thomson objected to Philly, a name that Burns defended strongly in another letter:

I remember your objections to the name Philly, but it is now the common abbreviation of Phillis, which is now a common christian name, Nelly, & Sally, the only name that suits, has to my ear, a vulgarity about them, which unfits them for any thing except burlesque.

PHILLY AND WILLY

He
O Philly, happy be that day
When roving through the gather'd hay,
My youthfu' heart was stown away,
And by thy charms, my Philly.

She
O Willy, ay I bless the grove
Where first I own'd my maiden love,
Whilst thou did pledge the Powers above
To be my ain dear Willy.

He
As songster of the early year
Are ilka day mair sweet to hear,
So ilka day to me mair dear
And charming is my Philly.

She
As on the brier the budding rose
Still richer breathes and fairer blows,
So in my tender bosom grows
The love I bear my Willy.

He
The milder sun and bluer sky
That crown my harvest cares wi' joy,
Were ne'er sae welcome to my eye
As is a sight o' Philly.

She
The little swallow's wanton wing,
Tho' wafting o'er the flowery Spring,
Did ne'er to me, sic tydings bring,
As meeting o' my Willy.

He
The bee that thro' the sunny hour
Sips nectar in the opening flower,
Compar'd wi' my delight is poor,
Upon the lips o' Philly.

She
The woodbine in the dewy weet
When evening shades in silence meet,
Is nocht sae fragrant or sae sweet
As is a kiss o' Willy.

He
Let Fortune's wheel at random run;
And Fools may tyne, and Knaves may win;
My thoughts are a' bound up on ane,
And that's my ain dear Philly.

She
What's a' the joys that gowd can gi'e?
I care na wealth a single flie;
The lad I love's the lad for me,
And that's my ain dear Willy.

stown = stolen; ilka = each; tyne = get lost; gowd = gold

Katy

Many are at odds over the identity of Katy, with some claiming that the name was altered from Betty and could therefore be Elizabeth Riddell. However, as the song was composed so soon after the exchange of letters between Burns and Thomson regarding names, it is highly possible that this could have been an attempt to compose a song with Mrs Katherine Thomson as the subject.

CANST THOU LEAVE ME THUS, MY KATY

Chorus
Canst thou leave me thus, my Katy?
Canst thou leave me thus, my Katy?
Well thou know'st my aching heart,
And canst thou leave me thus for pity?

Is this thy plighted, fond regard,
Thus cruelly to part, my Katy?
Is this thy faithful swain's reward,
An aching broken heart, my Katy?

Farewell! and ne'er such sorrows tear
That fickle heart of thine, my Katy!
Thou mayest find those will love thee dear,
But not a love like mine, my Katy.

Nanie

In a letter to Clarinda, Burns praised her for one particular line in a poem that she had sent to him and promised to use it at some future date in one of his own compositions. It is arguable whether or not this piece is the one, but this extract from a letter to Clarinda refers to the line.

It is perhaps rather wrong to speak highly to a friend of his letters; it is apt to lay one under a little restraint in their future letters, and restraint is the death of a friendly epistle, but there is one passage of your last charming letter, Thomson or Shenstone never exceeded it, nor often came up to it. I shall certainly steal it, and set it in some future poetic production, and get immortal fame by it. 'Tis when you bid the scenes of Nature remind you of Clarinda. Can I forget you, Clarinda? I would detest myself as a tasteless, unfeeling, insipid, infamous Blockhead! I have lov'd women of ordinary merit whom I could have loved forever. You are the first, the only unexceptionable individual of the beauteous Sex that I ever met with, and never woman more intirely possessed my soul. I know myself, and how far I can depend on passions, well. It has been my particular study …

He then refers to an item which she is having made by a jeweller for him:

I want it for a breast-pin to wear next my heart. I propose to keep sacred set times to wander in the woods and wilds for meditation on you. Then, and only then, your lovely image shall be produced to the day, with a reverence akin to Devotion …

MY NANIE'S AWA

Now in her green mantle blythe Nature arrays,
And listens the lambkins that bleat o'er the braes,
While birds warble welcomes in ilka green shaw;
But to me it's delightless – my Nanie's awa.

The snawdrap and primrose our woodlands adorn,
The violets bathe in the weet o' the morn;
They pain my sad bosom, sae sweetly they blaw,
They mind me o' Nanie – and Nanie's awa.

Thou lavrock that springs frae the dews of the lawn,
The shepherd to warn o' the grey-breaking dawn,
And thou mellow mavis that hails the night-fa',
Give over for pity – my Nanie's awa.

Come Autumn, sae pensive, in yellow and grey,
And soothe me wi' tydins o' Nature's decay;
The dark, dreary Winter, and wild-driving snaw,
Alane can delight me – now Nanie's awa.

ilka = every; shaw = wood; lavrock = lark

Jeany Scott

During the course of his Excise duties Burns found himself snowbound in the village of Ecclefechan. He found time to write to Thomson describing the situation and as he was obviously bored he penned a few lines about the daughter of the postmaster on a window. The letter is amusing as it describes his agonies at having to endure the playing of a fiddler in the inn.

My dear Thomson,
You cannot have any idea of the predicament in which I write you. In the course of my duty
as Supervisor (in which capacity I have acted of late) I came yesternight to this unfortunate,
wicked, little village.
I have gone forward but snows of ten feet deep have impeded my progress. I have tried to
'gae back the gate I cam again,' but the same obstacle has shut me up within insuperable bars.
To add to my misfortune; since dinner, a Scraper has been torturing Catgut, in sounds that
would have insulted the dying agonies of a Sow under the hands of a Butcher, and thinks
himself, on that very account, exceeding good company. In fact I have been in a dilemma,
either to get drunk, to forget these miseries, or to hang myself to get rid of these miseries, like
a prudent man (a character congenial to my every thought, word & deed) I, of two evils
have chosen the least, & am very drunk ... at your service ...

EPIGRAM ON MISS JEAN SCOTT

Oh! had each Scot of ancient times,
Been Jeany Scott, as thou art,
The bravest heart on English ground,
Had yielded like a coward.

The Lass o' Inverness

This is a story of the aftermath of the Battle of Culloden when the Duke of Cumberland ordered the massacre of hundreds of Jacobite soldiers who lay dying and injured on the battlefield. The relentless pursuit and murder of those who had escaped the field, along with their entire families, was carried out with a similar bloodthirsty zeal. The bodies were buried in mounds on the moor, and one can still sense the pervading eeriness that emanates from Culloden Moor today. The flower, Sweet William, was named after William, Duke of Cumberland, but is better known in Scotland as Stinking Billy. To this day it remains unpopular in Scottish households.

THE LOVELY LASS O' INVERNESS

The lovely lass o' Inverness,
Nae joy nor pleasure can she see;
For e'en and morn she cries, Alas!
And ay the saut tear blins her e'e;
Drumossie moor, Drumossie day,
A waefu' day it was to me;
For there I lost my father dear,
My father dear and brethren three!

Their winding-sheet the bludy clay,
Their graves are growing green to see;
And by them lies the dearest lad
That ever blest a woman's e'e!
Now wae to thee, thou cruel lord,
A bludy man I trow thou be;
For mony a heart thou has made sair,
That ne'er did wrang to thine or thee!

saut = salt; waefu' = sad; winding-sheet = shroud; bludy = bloody

Jessy Lewars

Jessy Lewars, an 18-year-old close neighbour of the Burns family in Dumfries, was also the daughter of one of the Bard's colleagues in the Excise. Burns was by now following his doctor's orders and immersing himself in the freezing waters of the Brow Well. Jessy was deeply involved in assisting with his nursing as well as caring for his children, as Jean was in confinement awaiting the birth of her ninth. The Burns family was very dependent on Jessy at this time. But even at this stage in his life, hardly able to move, and in constant need of care, he still managed, incredibly, to produce poems depicting young Jessy as a lover.

HERE'S A HEALTH TO ANE I LO'E DEAR

Chorus
Here's a health to ane I lo'e dear,
Here's a health to ane I lo'e dear;
Thou art sweet as the smile when fond lovers meet,
And soft as their parting tear – Jessy.

Although you maun may never be mine,
Although even hope is denied;
'Tis sweeter for thee despairing,
Than aught in the warld beside – Jessy.

I mourn thro' the gay, gaudy day,
As, hopeless, I muse on thy charms;
But welcome the dream of sweet slumber,
For then I am lockt in thy arms – Jessy.

He continued to write short verses in her honour. The first of them was supposedly written on the back of a hand-bill advertising 'A Grand Menagerie of Wild Beasts Alive'.

THE MENAGERIE

Talk not to me of savages
From Afric's burning sun,
No savage e'er can rend my heart
As Jessy, thou hast done.

But Jessy's lovely hand in mine,
A mutual faith to plight,
Not even to view the heavenly choir
Would be so blest a sight.

THE TOAST

Fill me with the rosy wine,
Call a toast – a toast divine;
Give the Poet's darling flame,
Lovely Jessy be the name;
Then thou mayest freely boast,
Thou hast given a peerless toast.

JESSY'S ILLNESS

Say, sages, what's the charm on earth
Can turn Death's dart aside?
It is not purity and worth,
Else Jessy had not died.

HER RECOVERY

But rarely seen since Nature's birth,
The natives of the sky;
Yet still one seraph's left on earth,
For Jessy did not die.

In March 1796 Burns wrote to James Johnson asking for a set of the *Scots Musical Museum* which he wished to present to Jessy Lewars:

I am ashamed to ask another favor of you because you have been so very good already, but my wife has a very particular friend of hers, a young lady who sings well, to whom she wishes to present the Scots Musical Museum, *if you have a spare copy, will you be so obliging as to send it by the very first Fly, as I am anxious to have it soon.*

Johnson duly sent the books as requested and Burns inscribed them with the following words:

Thine be the volumes, Jessy fair,
And with them take the poet's prayer;
That fate may in her fairest page,
With every kindliest, best presage,
Of future bliss, enroll thy name;
With native worth, and spotless fame,
And wakeful caution still aware

Of ill – but chief, man's felon snare;
All blameless joys on earth we find,
And all the treasures of the mind –
These be thy guardian and reward;
So prays thy faithful friend, the Bard.

Dumfries, June 26th 1796, Robert Burns.

Afterword

Less than a month after inscribing the volumes to Jessy Lewars, Robert Burns died. On 25 July 1796 Dumfries was overwhelmed by the thousands of Scots who poured into the town to attend his funeral. It was a very grand affair, for in his later years Robert Burns had enlisted in the Dumfries Volunteers, a military group formed as part of the national defence against any possible French invasion.

His comrades in the Volunteers fired three volleys of shots over his coffin and Burns was laid to rest in St Michael's Kirkyard. His wife, Jean Armour, was not in attendance as she was that day engaged in giving birth to the latest addition to the Burns family. Their son, Maxwell, named after the doctor who had unwittingly condemned Burns to an early death, chose the day of his father's funeral to enter the world.

Even in death Burns was not allowed to lie in peace. The Scottish nation gradually woke up to the magnitude of their loss and eventually his remains were taken from his simple grave and placed in a much grander mausoleum in the far corner of St Michael's where they now rest.

However, it was not only Scotland that mourned the loss of the Bard. More monuments and statues to his memory have been erected in countries around the world than to any other writer in history. Whether he would have approved of all this can only be conjecture, for although he fought to have a memorial erected in Edinburgh to another Scottish poet, Robert Fergusson, Burns was scornful of the rich and their grand monuments and memorials.

Go to your sculptor'd tombs, ye Great,
In a' the tinsel trash o' state.

Robert Burns, as we have now ascertained through the content of the many poems and letters in the foregoing pages, was indeed a man of great passion. Coupled with that passion was an extraordinary tenderness and a need to be loved as well as to love.

He doubtless enjoyed and revelled in the physical side of love, but his words tell us that to him, love was far more than that. Love, to Robert Burns, was the meeting of minds and souls. First and last, he was indeed a true romantic.

Index of First Lines